Pump some spiritual iron.

Physical fitness is big today. We spend a fair amount of time trying to improve and strengthen these mortal bodies of ours. And God approves. Perfect worship includes the care and respect of our bodies for they, too, along with the mind and spirit, are part of God's divine creation. But more importantly, your body should express outwardly your inward spirituality and reflect God's holiness. Do you know how to achieve *spiritual* fitness?

Terry Fullam's *Fit for God's Presence*—the new, expanded edition of *Your Body, God's Temple* — shows you point by point the best ways to develop all the parts of your spiritual body—your ears and eyes, for just two examples. You will find "warm-up exercises"— some introspective questions particularly insightful for group study; and "stretching" exercises—pertinent memory verses to help you tone up to be your best for God.

Make *Fit for God's Presence* your own spiritual fitness program! You can reach your goal of building up your spirit *now* for a life that will be spent eternally reflecting glory on our Creator.

FIT FOR GOD'S PRESENCE

FIT FOR GOD'S PRESENCE

Everett L. (Jerry) Fullam

Published by
chosen books

FLEMING H. REVELL COMPANY
OLD TAPPAN, NEW JERSEY

Scripture texts are from the Holy Bible, New International Version, copyright © 1973, 1978, 1984 International Bible Society. Used by permission of Zondervan Bible Publishers.

Library of Congress Cataloging in Publication Data

Fullam, Everett L.
  Fit for God's presence / by Everett L. (Terry) Fullam.
      p.   cm.
  ISBN 0-8007-9148-7
      1. Body, Human—Religious aspects—Christianity.   2. Spiritual
  life—Anglican authors.   I. Title.
  BT741.2.F83   1989
  248.2—dc20   89-34448
                                                                            CIP

A Chosen Book
Copyright © 1989 by Everett L. Fullam

Chosen Books are published by
Fleming H. Revell Company
Old Tappan, New Jersey
Printed in the United States of America

For Ruth, my wife of 36 years;
Our children, Everett and Rosemary,
Melanie and Charles,
and Andrea

One of the constants of the Christian life is that we are always in the process of change and growth. Our Lord edits and revises as He chooses to unfold the plot of our lives. So it is with things we have written; editing, revision, and updating are needed periodically.

Seven of the teachings included in this book were originally published in 1978 under the title *Your Body, God's Temple*. In the fall of 1988, Jane Campbell, Editor of Chosen Books, who had worked on the previous book, called to explore the idea of an updated, expanded version. She rightly felt that there were many current issues in the church and the world that these principles would address.

My assistant, Lynda Barnes, took it from there. She researched appropriate additional material, and then reworked both existing and new content within the framework of a study guide as Jane had suggested. Lastly, the eagle eyes of Ruth Malloy and Alta Jelliffe checked for all sorts of human errors.

The result of their combined talents is in your hands. I give thanks to God for their dedication and diligence, and pray that the new edition will be as great a blessing to you as it was to me.

Terry Fullam
Pentecost, 1989

Contents

FIT FOR GOD'S PRESENCE

1

Body Fitness

Have you ever wondered why people bow their heads and close their eyes when they pray? Why some Christians kneel in church? Why some make the sign of the cross or genuflect? Why some raise their hands? All these are physical expressions of spiritual realities.

Bowing the head, kneeling, genuflecting—all are postures of submission to and reverence for God. Some people make the sign of the cross because they identify with the crucifixion of Jesus Christ; the cross is the symbol of death to self and resurrection to new life. Some people raise their hands because, according to Scripture, the most ancient posture of prayer is standing before the Lord with hands upraised. That's also the universal posture of surrender, and I think there is none more appropriate for us to assume in the presence of the Lord. We worship with outward expressions of our inward beliefs, because we are not just spiritual but embodied beings.

We think of worship as a spiritual reality, but some people who have grasped this truth have lost a complementary truth. They say that if worship is principally spiritual and therefore inward, what we do with our physical bodies is unimportant. Yet the apostle Paul articulated the relationship between the physical and the spiritual in this way: "Do you not know that your body is a temple of the Holy Spirit, who is in you, whom you have received from God? You are not your own; you were

bought at a price" (1 Corinthians 6:19–20a). Paul's inevitable conclusion: "Therefore honor God with your body."

Perhaps the reason some people have difficulty with
this concept is that they don't consider their bodies—their
physical beings—fit for God's presence. They have lost the
sense of body, mind, and spirit united in the worship of
God and have mentally separated their worship of God
from their bodies.

What God has joined together, we separate at our peril!
I want to talk about our need to respect our bodies, to
understand their creation; what we are to do and not do
with the bodies we have; and how we are to understand
our physical decline. People today spend hours of their
time, great percentages of their money, and huge amounts
of their energy on physical fitness, often ignoring the most
important fitness requirement in their lives—being fit for
God's presence.

Following are four principles that are vital to any person
seeking spiritual fitness.

Principle One: Respect Your Body

I am told by those in my parish involved in various
forms of physical fitness that the first step to making a
change is gaining a respect for our bodies. This means
gaining an understanding of the way our physical selves
work and working with that understanding to improve,
not destroy, our bodies. It begins with a checkup, a way to
measure various functions to see where they are and what
needs improving.

This applies spiritually as well. The spiritual reason we
are to respect our bodies relates to the nature of God. The
primary biblical characteristic of our God is that He is
absolutely holy. Some of the pagan gods of the Romans
and the Greeks were considered powerful, as is our own
God in infinite measure. Some were thought knowledge-
able; our God is omniscient. But the God of Abraham,

Isaac, and Jacob, the God of Israel, the God and Father of our Lord Jesus Christ is distinguished by His holiness. If we begin with this understanding, we know we will all be in need of improvement!

Do you remember the vision of the prophet Isaiah? He saw the Lord God high and lifted up, seated upon a throne, and he heard the seraphim singing, "Holy, holy, holy is the Lord Almighty; the whole earth is full of his glory" (Isaiah 6:3b). Many hundreds of years later, the apostle John wrote, "This is the message we have heard from him and declare to you: God is light; in him there is no darkness at all" (1 John 1:5). There are no shadowy places, no dark aspects in the being and the character of God. John goes on to say, "If we claim to have fellowship with him yet walk in the darkness, we lie and do not live by the truth. But if we walk in the light, as he is in the light, we have fellowship with one another" (verses 6–7a).

We cannot have fellowship with a holy God and walk in an unholy fashion; it is as simple as that. The character of God defines the kind of relationship we must have with Him, and it is precisely because God is holy that His people must be holy, too. Two obscure texts in the Old Testament help to establish the connection between God as a holy God and His call to us to be a holy people: "The Lord said to Moses, 'Speak to the entire assembly of Israel and say to them: "Be holy because I, the Lord your God, am holy" ' " (Leviticus 19:1–2); and "Moses then said to Aaron, 'This is what the Lord spoke of when he said: "Among those who approach me I will show myself holy; in the sight of all the people I will be honored" ' " (Leviticus 10:3).

Later on in Leviticus, God adds a peculiar command: "Do not cut your bodies for the dead or put tattoo marks on yourselves. I am the Lord" (Leviticus 19:28). The first part of that verse forbids a pagan practice of cutting the body and bleeding to express mourning at the death of a loved one. But perhaps you didn't know that tattoos are also forbidden in Scripture. Why? Because our God is a holy God, and our bodies are to be holy to the Lord.

The following verse was addressed to the priests of Israel with reference to the people: "Priests must not shave their heads or shave off the edges of their beards or cut their bodies. They must be holy to their God and must not profane the name of their God" (Leviticus 21:5–6a).

It is clear that in the eyes of the Lord, to mark the physical body is to attack the honor and glory of God, since we were created in His image. This idea is continued in the New Testament: "As obedient children, do not conform to the evil desires you had when you lived in ignorance. But just as he who called you is holy, so be holy in all you do; for it is written: 'Be holy, because I am holy' " (1 Peter 1:14–16).

The reason we are to respect our bodies is that we were created by a holy God to be a holy people. To mark and deface the body is as inappropriate as to mark or deface someone else's property. To abuse the bodies God has given us is a sin in His sight.

Today the abuse of the body through various forms of addictive substances (drugs, alcohol, nicotine) is the number one problem we face in our society. These abuses lead to many other problems, ranging from the high cost of health insurance to robberies and broken families, all the way to violence and murder. As bad as those incidents are, they are only symptoms of a society that has lost its understanding of the need for a relationship with God, lost its sense of His holiness and our own. I don't think that any amount of money and muscle can clear up society's problems until people are able to get to know God and reach out to Him. It has been statistically proven that the programs with the greatest success rate are those that advocate dependence on one outside of the individual. AA calls it the "higher power"; Christians know His name.

Principle Two: Know Your Limit

After the checkup is completed, we have a picture of what we can and can't do in a physical fitness program. We learn our limitations. The same is true spiritually. While we were created by God in His image, our bodies were created of the dust of the earth. The first chapter of Genesis describes the account of creation—that it was accomplished over a period of time in a sequence that accords with today's best scientific knowledge. Then on the sixth day of creation: "God said, 'Let us make man in our image, in our likeness, and let them rule over the fish of the sea and the birds of the air, over the livestock, over all the earth, and over all the creatures that move along the ground.' So God created man in his own image, in the image of God he created him; male and female he created them" (Genesis 1:26–27).

Man and woman appeared at the end of God's creative activity, and after God created man and woman, He rested. The pronoun *us* in the phrase *Let us make man* sets apart God's decision to create mankind from His decision to create everything else on earth. On the first five days of creation, God said, "Let there be." The Bible describes creation that was spoken into being. But something different occurred with the creation of humanity. Man and woman were created in God's image.

When the Bible says we were created in the image of God, however, it does not mean that we resemble Him physically. Jesus Himself told us that God is Spirit. Being made in God's image means that we were created in God's "class." We are not God, nor are we a part of God. We were created in His class, so that we might sustain a relationship with Him.

At home I have a large white Angora cat named Magnificat. I love him very much, and he in turn responds to me with a certain degree of affection—at times! But there is a limit to the possibilities in our relationship, because cats are in a different class of creation from humans. There are similarities between cat bodies and human bodies. Cats have a respiratory system, as do humans. We have similar digestive and reproductive systems, because we were made to inhabit a common environment. He can eat some of the food I enjoy, and if I were truly desperate I could digest the food he regularly eats. But there is a limit to what we can share. I can care for my cat and love him, but I cannot really communicate with him because he is of a different order of beings altogether.

When you and I were created in the image of God, we were created with the capacity of sustaining a relationship with Him. We can commune with Him spirit to Spirit. Furthermore, God created us as moral beings, knowing the difference between right and wrong, and He gave us the freedom to choose one over the other. All of that is part of what it means to be created in God's image.

It is not particularly in our physical bodies that we bear the image of God. Genesis 2:7 describes how we were created: "And the Lord God formed man from the dust of the ground and breathed into his nostrils the breath of life, and man became a living being." *Formed . . . from the dust of the ground* is a simple way of saying that our physical bodies contain the same physical elements found in the natural creation. The body reveals traces of minerals and other elements found in creation—in the dust of the earth. Should that surprise you when it's proven scientifically, remember that it is what the Bible says! We can do whatever we want to improve ourselves—go to the gym and work out, jog, go to the hairdresser, use cosmetics—but underneath it all we are simply dust. One day that will be evident.

On Ash Wednesday it is common for folk in churches of Catholic tradition to receive an imposition of ashes, usually on the forehead. As the ashes are applied, the priest or minister says to the person, "Remember that you are dust, and to dust you shall return." Why do we do that?

We are recalling the words of the Lord to Adam after the Fall: "By the sweat of your brow you will eat your food until you return to the ground, since from it you were taken; for dust you are and to dust you will return" (Genesis 3:19). The imposition of ashes reminds us that our bodies are created from the dust of the earth. It reminds us of our mortality.

The book of Job makes a corollary point that reminds us how dependent we are on God, not only for our creation, but for our day-to-day survival. After suggesting that God gave mankind charge over the earth (to care for it, not destroy it!) Job says, "If it were his intention and he withdrew his spirit and breath, all mankind would perish together and man would return to the dust" (34:14–15).

The Hebrew word for *breath*—*ruach*—is exactly the same as the word for *spirit*, as when we read in Genesis that God breathed into man the spirit, or breath, of life. A classic creed of the Church says, "We believe in the Holy Spirit, the Lord, the giver of life," because the Spirit of God gives the life of God. The Trinity—the "us" in "Let us make man in our image"—was present at the creation of man. According to the passage in Job, therefore, if God were to withdraw His Spirit, mankind would perish and return to the dust, confirming that the body is inhabited by the *ruach*, the spirit, or breath, of God. The human body is "inspired"; it has received breath into itself. When a person dies, we say he or she has expired, meaning that the spirit or breath has gone out of the body. We are dependent upon God for our very life!

One final Scripture passage puts this mortality into divine perspective: "As a father has compassion on his children, so the Lord has compassion on those who fear him; for he knows how we are formed, he remembers that we are dust" (Psalm 103:13–14).

The psalmist is saying that God pities us—not in a condescending way, as one stranger might another, but in an empathic way, as a father might identify with his child.

He does this because He remembers that we are made of dust. God knows our limitations; He has put them there. It is we who must discover them at the start of our quest for spiritual fitness.

Our bodies are dust. They wear out, and one day we will lay them aside, but that does not mean they are not significant.

Alistair Cooke, an Englishman who has been living in America for decades, knows this country as few natives do and is able to see it from a different point of view. In his book *America* he points out one item that we in our disposable society take for granted to the astonishment of people abroad—the paper towel. It seems so massively wasteful to non-Americans to use paper as a towel and just throw it away!

We must avoid having the paper towel mentality toward our bodies. They may be made of dust, but they are still the temples of the Holy Spirit, made in the image of a holy God, so it matters how we treat them.

Principle Three: Commit Yourself

In the quest for physical fitness, many people join health clubs that offer a variety of options to move them toward the goal of fitness. Most of these clubs require some sort of commitment for a specific period of time to receive the maximum physical benefit. For some, such a commitment is a sacrifice of other priorities in life, in order to gain something of lasting value.

A similar commitment is asked of those seeking to be made fit for God's presence. "For from him and through him and to him are all things. To him be the glory forever! Amen. Therefore, I urge you, brothers, in view of God's mercy, to offer your bodies as living sacrifices, holy and pleasing to God—which is your spiritual worship" (Romans 11:36–12:1).

What constitutes spiritual worship acceptable to God? We are called upon to give our bodies back to the Lord as living sacrifices. The image for worship here is exterior and physical as well as internal and spiritual. Many have one or two spiritual exercises that they do well. If you think of church participation as a spiritual health club, you'll get the idea. Folk may come into church on a Sunday morning and stand and sing the hymns, read the prayers, receive the Communion, but they are not necessarily worshiping God. Mouthing a liturgy is not worship. Listening to a great choir sing soaring anthems is not worship. Listening to a great preacher preach a powerful sermon is not worship. A generous contribution to the offering plate or hours spent in volunteer service to the church are not worship either. Unless we first offer ourselves to God, none of these things counts; we have not worshiped at all.

A member of my congregation once remarked, "The problem with living sacrifices is they keep getting down from the altar!" It's true, yet no one else can worship for us. Your clergyman can't do it for you. Your spouse can't; your parents can't; and you can't do it for your children. Worship is one's own offering of one's life to the Lord.

You can be an island of resistance in the midst of a worshiping people. No one else would ever know, as you might sing lustily, kneel with great piety, pray fervently. But you know, and God knows, since, as many Christians hear every Sunday, our God is a God "unto whom all hearts are open, all desires known, and from whom no secrets are hid." We are to worship God with our bodies as living sacrifices.

What would it mean to offer our bodies as living sacrifices? For one thing, it would mean that we don't follow the urges of our bodies. Various appetites tempt us constantly. Does this sound familiar? " 'Everything is permissible for me'—but not everything is beneficial. 'Everything is permissible for me'—but I will not be mastered by anything. 'Food for the stomach and the stomach for food'—but God will destroy them both" (1 Corinthians 6:12–13a). We are to master our desires, not be mastered by them. What we are especially not to do with our bodies, according to the New Testament, is indulge in any kind of sexual immorality or impurity. Paul goes on to say, "The body is not meant for sexual immorality, but for the Lord, and the Lord for the body" (verse 13b).

He continues:

> Do you not know that your bodies are members of Christ himself? Shall I then take the members of Christ and unite them with a prostitute? Never! Do you not know that he who unites himself with a prostitute is one with her in body? For it is said, "The two will become one flesh." But he who unites himself with the Lord is one with him in spirit.
>
> Flee from sexual immorality. All other sins a man commits are outside his body, but he who sins sexually sins against his own body.   verses 15–18

One of our biggest problems as human beings is managing our sexuality. It's not easy, and it's getting more difficult as the society we live in lowers its standards day by day. The prevailing philosophy—"It's my body; I can do anything I please with it as long as I don't hurt anyone"—fails to grasp a truth about our physical beings: They are a part of Christ. The apostle goes on in verse 19: "Do you not know that your body is a temple of the Holy Spirit, who is in you, whom you have received from God? You are not your own; you were bought at a price. Therefore honor God with your body."

Think of the most beautiful church buildings you can imagine—such as the great cathedrals of Europe. Although these buildings may still be consecrated to the worship of God, when the services are over, the people leave and the doors are closed. God no more dwells in them than He does in the streets in front of them. The Church, the New Testament tells us, is not a building; it's a people. We don't go to a church, we are the Church. The Lord God has chosen to dwell in the hearts and lives of His people, not in buildings erected in His name. We are not God or even a little part of God; that is a pagan teaching. But if we have come to Jesus Christ and made a commitment to Him in faith, we are the temples of God because His Holy Spirit dwells within us.

Can you see, then, that taking our bodies and misusing them sexually is defacing the temple of God? To use our sexuality in a way that neither God's law nor His love allows is to desecrate the temple of God, just as surely as if an immoral sexual act were committed on the high altar of a cathedral.

There has been much public controversy in the Church about determining a wrong or right use of the gift of sexuality. Many are clamoring for the Church to bless that which God has declared anathema. There have been emotional, divisive, and ugly exchanges over this issue. It all comes down to one thing—commitment to the program, commitment to doing what we know is right for us out of obedience, even if it doesn't feel good or right to us at the time. We commit ourselves knowing that we'll get through the pain and come out better in the end.

The fact is, we are God's twice over. We first belong to Him by virtue of our creation. Then, when we fell away from God and acted as though we belonged to ourselves, God did not overthrow us in judgment as we deserved. Instead, He brought us back; He bought us back, Paul says, "at a price." It's just as we might buy back from a pawnshop something that had originally belonged to us but had been traded in for something else. God bought us back, and the price for our redemption was the death and resurrection of His only Son, Jesus. "For you know that it was not with perishable things such as silver or gold that you were redeemed from the empty way of life handed down to you from your forefathers, but with the precious blood of Christ, a lamb without blemish or defect" (1 Peter 1:18–19).

That redemption makes it possible for anyone to live a life pleasing to God, not be caught in the bondage of immorality. "You are not your own; you were bought at a price. Therefore honor God with your body" (1 Corinthians 6:19b–20).

Principle Four: Get Results

If we stick with a physical fitness program, the time comes when we reach our goal and there is cause for celebration. It is the same with spiritual fitness. With physical fitness, the goal is strengthening and prolonging the enjoyment of the physical existence. With spiritual fitness, the goal is strengthening the spirit now for a life that continues after the physical life ends. The clear statement of Genesis 3, "Dust you are and to dust you will return," teaches that our physical bodies will decompose over a period of time. The Christian teaching is that the dust returns to the earth as it was, and the spirit returns to God, who gave it.

Our spiritual beings can decompose while we live in great physical strength, and our spiritual bodies can strengthen as our physical selves decline. I'm sure you can think of examples of people who glory in their physical selves and have little thought for their spiritual lives. Have you ever known someone who groaned with the weariness of the flesh? Perhaps you've never thought of it as a longing to be clothed with a new body. The physical body tires, breaks down, and needs periodic repair. We are constantly made aware of its frailty. We ultimately long for something more permanent and eternal.

In a remarkable passage in the New Testament, the body is described as a tent:

Now we know that if the earthly tent we live in is destroyed, we have a building from God, an eternal house in heaven, not built by human hands. Meanwhile we groan, longing to be clothed with our heavenly dwelling, because when we are clothed, we will not be found naked. For while we are in this tent, we groan and are burdened, because we do not wish to be unclothed but to be clothed with our heavenly dwelling, so that what is mortal may be swallowed up by life. Now it is God who has made us for this very purpose and has given us the Spirit as a deposit, guaranteeing what is to come.   2 Corinthians 5:1–5

What awaits a person when he or she dies? Paul addresses this in 1 Corinthians 15:

But someone may ask, "How are the dead raised? With what kind of body will they come?" How foolish! What you sow does not come to life unless it dies. When you sow, you do not plant the body that will be, but just a seed, perhaps of wheat or of something else. But God gives it a body as he has determined, and to each kind of seed he gives its own body. . . .
So will it be with the resurrection of the dead. The body that is sown is perishable, it is raised imperishable; it is sown in dishonor, it is raised in glory; it is sown in weakness, it is raised in power; it is sown a natural body, it is raised a spiritual body.   verses 35–38, 42–44a

Not a disembodied state; human beings are not destined to become unclothed spiritual beings flitting about eternity. Rather, the person's spirit returns to the Lord to be clothed with a glorified body, related to his or her present body as a seed is related to fruit. This does not mean that corpses will be resuscitated or that the physical bodies we now inhabit will be "reassembled" atom for atom. Instead, we will receive new bodies, fashioned perfectly to express the spirits within.

The Bible promises these new bodies beginning in the

book of Job, which some think was written even before the
book of Genesis. "I know that my Redeemer lives, and
that in the end he will stand upon the earth. And after my
skin has been destroyed, yet in my flesh I will see God; I
myself will see him with my own eyes—I, and not
another. How my heart yearns within me!" (Job 19:25–27).

Yearning to be fit for God's presence! As a dwelling
place for the Holy Spirit, we are not our own; we were
made for eternity. Our earthly bodies, unable to withstand
the ravages of time, will one day put on immortality, and
we will be as we are to be and see Him as He is. The
apostle John writes, "Dear friends, now we are children of
God, and what we will be has not yet been made known.
But we know that when he appears, we shall be like him,
for we shall see him as he is"(1 John 3:2).

Summary

Until that happens we can concentrate on the steps
toward spiritual fitness. Created in the image of God, we
are intended to reflect His holiness, not only in our spirits
for eternity but also in our bodies here on earth. We can
use our bodies as we choose, for our own purposes, or we
can do as Paul asked in Romans 12: Present them to God
as living sacrifices, as lives filled with acts of spiritual
worship.

Just how we go about doing that is the subject of the
studies ahead.

Warm-Up Exercises

1. If you respected your body as God intended you to,
   how would things change in your life?

2. Are there patterns or habits in your life that go beyond
   the limits God has set?

3. What expressions of your worship would others see in you if you were a living sacrifice to God?

4. What kind of spiritual seed do you have? What do you imagine your resurrection body will be like? Is it fit for God's presence?

Stretching

Commit 1 Corinthians 6:19b–20 to memory and live it out each day: "You are not your own; you were bought at a price. Therefore honor God with your body."

2

Eyes to See

In Proverbs there is a straightforward statement that at first glance is so obvious, we might wonder why it is included: "Ears that hear and eyes that see—the Lord has made them both" (20:12).

Yet on second thought, we realize that not all people with ears hear and not all people with eyes see. So it is with our spiritual eyes. Spiritual blindness is a far deeper problem than physical blindness. The Lord Jesus made that point clear when He performed a healing miracle on a blind man's eyes.

> As he went along, he saw a man blind from birth. His disciples asked him, "Rabbi, who sinned, this man or his parents, that he was born blind?"
>
> "Neither this man nor his parents sinned," said Jesus, "but this happened so that the work of God might be displayed in his life. As long as it is day, we must do the work of him who sent me. Night is coming, when no one can work. While I am in the world, I am the light of the world."
>
> Having said this, he spit on the ground, made some mud with the saliva, and put it on the man's eyes. "Go," he told him, "wash in the pool of Siloam" (this word means Sent). So the man went and washed, and came home seeing. John 9:1–7

Spiritual Blindness

The man was delivered from physical blindness. Standing nearby were the religious leaders of the day who suffered from a far worse fate—blindness of the spirit—though they would not admit it.

> They brought to the Pharisees the man who had been blind. Now the day on which Jesus had made the mud and opened the man's eyes was a Sabbath. Therefore the Pharisees also asked him how he had received his sight. "He put mud on my eyes," the man replied, "and I washed, and now I see."
> Some of the Pharisees said, "This man is not from God, for he does not keep the Sabbath."
> But others asked, "How can a sinner do such miraculous signs?" So they were divided.   verses 13–16

The Pharisees are still with us today. They represent those religious professionals who are more concerned with tradition and ritualistic precision than with healing the people or seeing that they are brought to an understanding of the truth. In another instance recorded in Mark, Jesus told the Pharisees, "The Sabbath was made for man, not man for the Sabbath" (Mark 2:27). In other words, "Let's keep things in their proper perspective"; God cares for His people first!

How tragic that some of God's greatest enemies are found among the religious institutions! What makes it so difficult for them to see the mighty acts of God? Perhaps they have a particular stand to maintain or a theological ax to grind. Or they think they have been given power to control God as though He were a genie in a bottle awaiting their wishes. Maybe they consider themselves God's patrons, with advisory rights over Him that come with such sponsorship. It is to them as well as to His disciples that Jesus would say, "As long as it is day, we must do the work of Him who sent Me."

Today's Pharisees are attempting to include in Christian doctrine other beliefs and thoughts that Jesus came to correct. Much of what is called New Age is nothing but old paganism in various forms. Still others are claiming "new revelations" since Jesus' return to the Father. The all-roads-to-God theory is being proclaimed from pulpits in many denominations of the Church that bears the name of the One who said, "No one comes to the Father except through me" (John 14:6b). Some are even trying to call the Father "the Mother." Jesus warned of this when He said, "The night is coming." The world has always wanted to avoid the truth.

> Finally they turned again to the blind man, "What have you to say about him? It was your eyes he opened."
> The man replied, "He is a prophet."
> The Jews still did not believe that he had been blind and had received his sight until they sent for the man's parents. "Is this your son?" they asked. "Is this the one you say was born blind? How is it that now he can see?"
> "We know he is our son," the parents answered, "and we know he was born blind. But how he can see now, or who opened his eyes, we don't know. Ask him. He is of age; he will speak for himself." His parents said this because they were afraid of the Jews, for already the Jews had decided that anyone who acknowledged that Jesus was the Christ would be put out of the synagogue.
> John 9:17–22

Wouldn't you think that the man's parents would have been overjoyed by this healing miracle and given full credit where it was due? But they were afraid, and fear often robs people of their ability to give a truthful witness. They weigh what they would lose if they told the truth against what they would gain or keep by their silence. Stilling the voice of testimony ultimately clouds the eye of faith—making it more difficult to see the hand of God at work.

The parents, neither denying the miracle nor confessing it as divine, put the burden of response back on their son.

> A second time they summoned the man who had been
> blind. "Give glory to God," they said. "We know this man
> is a sinner." He replied, "Whether he is a sinner or not, I
> don't know. One thing I do know. I was blind but now I
> see!"   verses 24–25

Seeing Is Believing

By the simple recounting of the man's experience, the Pharisees were thwarted in their attempt to discount the validity of Jesus' miracle. Sound logic or a clever argument might have been turned aside, but there is something compelling about the power of personal testimony. The most skeptical person in the world can protest that he has never experienced anything like your miracle or mine, but he cannot refute the reality of another person's life.

Another story recorded in Acts 4 demonstrates that same principle. After Peter and John healed a man who had been lame from birth, they were cast into prison and then questioned for having healed in Jesus' name. Following Peter's explanation is a powerful observation: "But since they could see the man who had been healed standing there with them, there was nothing they could say" (verse 14).

The mouths of the critics were closed by the evidence of a transformed life right before their eyes. The strongest evidence that the Church can offer to a confused, unbelieving world is a personal testimony. I think of the international ministries of Full Gospel Business Men's Fellowship and Women's Aglow, centered around the personal testimony of God's hand at work in the lives of His people today.

There are still (and always will be) those who, like the Pharisees in John 9, will resist the evidence of their physical senses due to the blindness of their spiritual eyes.

Then they asked him, "What did he do to you? How did he open your eyes?"

He answered, "I have told you already and you did not listen. Why do you want to hear it again? Do you want to become his disciples, too?"

Then they hurled insults at him and said, "You are this fellow's disciple! We are disciples of Moses! We know that God spoke to Moses, but as for this fellow, we don't even know where he comes from."   John 9:26–29

Believing Is Understanding

The Pharisees were claiming to be disciples of Moses and Scripture scholars, yet they did not understand that both Moses and the Scriptures pointed to Jesus. Centuries later, St. Augustine would sum up this problem by saying, "Do not seek to understand that you may believe, but believe, that you may understand."

I encountered a similar lack of understanding due to unbelief during my first year of graduate school at Harvard, where I studied New Testament under a world-famous scholar. After I exegeted a particular passage one day, he said, "Mr. Fullam, you're entirely right; what you've said is exactly what the passage says. I just don't believe it."

During the course of the semester, this professor, who had devoted his entire life to studying the New Testament, admitted he believed little of its content. Tragically, in the years since then more professors like him have inhabited the seminaries and graduate schools and ultimately changed the pulpits across the face of the Church. These people have studied Scripture as an ancient document yet never known the One of whom it speaks. The practice is currently known as biblical criticism—trying to disprove, rather than understand, the Scriptures.

Perhaps the most cogent comment regarding biblical criticism I ever heard came from a fellow priest, the Rev. Russell Burchard. Quoting a statement by Professor Luke

Johnson, who taught at Berkley Divinity School at Yale in the '70s: "The way we teach the New Testament is comparable to the rape of women." Fr. Burchard added, "It is comparable to rape because it takes the love act and perverts it to an act of violence, leaving its subject with neither power nor dignity."

Like some theologians today, if the Pharisees had truly been studying to learn about God, they would have recognized Jesus as the One of whom Moses spoke. The man healed of blindness declared this:

> "Now that is remarkable! You don't know where he comes from, yet he opened my eyes. We know that God does not listen to sinners. He listens to the godly man who does his will. Nobody has ever heard of opening the eyes of a man born blind. If this man were not from God, he could do nothing."
> To this they replied, "You were steeped in sin at birth; how dare you lecture us!" And they threw him out.
>
> John 9:30–34

In contrast to the Pharisees' spiritual blindness, the man who had been healed showed that his spiritual eyes had been opened as well as his physical eyes. First he had acknowledged "the man called Jesus." Then he called Him a "prophet," then a "man from God." Finally he declared his belief and worshiped Him:

> Jesus heard that they had thrown him out, and when he found him, he said, "Do you believe in the Son of Man?" "Who is he, sir?" the man asked. "Tell me so that I may believe in him." Jesus said, "You have now seen him; in fact, he is the one speaking with you." Then the man said, "Lord, I believe," and he worshiped him.   verses 35–38

Healing Faith or Faith Healing?

Don't miss another important point in this passage: God does not always wait for people to come to faith before He heals them. He may touch them when they don't yet know who Jesus is. They don't attribute their healing to God because they don't know Him. As their understanding increases, they might attribute it to a person of God's choosing, perhaps the person who laid hands upon them and prayed for them, as when the young man referred to Jesus as a prophet.

Finally, when they come to know the love of Jesus, they are able to acknowledge Him as Lord and to worship Him. God heals as He chooses, in the way and in the time that will ultimately bring Him the greatest results. Do you recall His words to His disciples at the beginning of the passage—that neither the man nor his parents had sinned? Jesus said that the blindness had "happened so that the work of God might be displayed." That's a hard truth for people to accept.

In recent years many ministries have taught that if we have enough faith, we can be healed. On top of their afflictions, people have become angry and spiritually wounded because they have felt they were not faith-filled enough or good enough to be healed; they felt they had been rejected by God in some way.

Nothing could be further from the truth. God desires healing for us all, and faith is the way to healing of body, mind, and spirit. But God sees the whole span of time and circumstances, and He knows the hearts of His people. He knows in what way His work will be displayed to the greatest number of eyes that will see and believe. Many have come to faith in God through the death of a loved one after much prayer for healing, while others have become bitter because their prayers went unanswered according to their desires. We don't like to face the fact that, for Christians, death is the ultimate healing: "Precious in the sight of the Lord is the death of his saints" (Psalm 116:15).

John 9, which begins with a mighty healing of physical blindness, concludes with Jesus' pointed discussion of spiritual blindness. "Jesus said, 'For judgment I have come into this world, so that the blind will see and those who see will become blind.' Some Pharisees who were with him heard him say this and asked, 'What? Are we blind too?' Jesus said, 'If you were blind, you would not be guilty of sin; but now that you claim you can see, your guilt remains' " (verses 39–41).

Deliberate Disobedience

How does it happen that many physically sighted people are spiritually blind? For some, the issue is ignorance; for others it is deliberate disobedience. Ignorance is simply not knowing, never having been told. I often tell people that they don't know until they know that they didn't know. Jesus says they are not guilty.

On the other hand, for those who should know better, the guilt remains until repentance. What forms might that deliberate disobedience take?

Unbelief

Let's start with unbelief. This is cited by the apostle Paul, who, after spending an entire day trying to convince a group of Romans about Jesus, said:

"The Holy Spirit spoke the truth to your forefathers when he said through Isaiah the prophet:
'Go to this people and say,
"You will be ever hearing but never understanding;
     you will be ever seeing but never perceiving."
For this people's heart has become calloused;
     they hardly hear with their ears,
     and they have closed their eyes.
Otherwise they might see with their eyes,
     hear with their ears,
     understand with their hearts
and turn and I would heal them.' "

Acts 28:25b–27

God can forgive the sin of unbelief if we repent and turn from it, but every time we resist the truth of the Holy Spirit, we take a step backward into darkness. It is as if spiritual cataracts were gradually building up, clouding our vision. If we persist in our unbelief, there comes a point where the laser surgery of the Holy Spirit will not work. It's not that God's mercy runs out; rather, God lets us close our eyes and go our own way. God is a gentleman; He never insists that we believe.

Rebellion

Rebellion is insistence on our own will, and we are all guilty of it to some degree from the time of our birth! One of the greatest challenges in the quests for both physical and spiritual fitness is the overcoming of the will. Ask anyone who's had to diet about willpower. Spiritual rebellion is deliberately acting contrary to the will and purposes of God. There is nothing ignorant about it; when we rebel we know exactly what we're doing. And when we do, the cataracts begin to form. We find an example of this in Ezekiel 12:1–2: "The word of the Lord came to me: 'Son of man, you are living among a rebellious people. They have eyes to see but do not see and ears to hear but do not hear, for they are a rebellious people.' "

The more we rebel, the less we are able to see. Our focus narrows. We see things filtered through our own desires, not clearly at all. It's a gradual process, and we hardly notice it for a while. At first it might prompt a twinge in our consciences, which perhaps we rationalize or justify. Soon we reach a point when it no longer bothers us at all. Scripture describes this as the searing, or the cauterizing, of the conscience, the hardening of the heart; it warns of a time to come when a person no longer possesses the ability to repent.

Turning Away

There is no person, however primitive, who does not regard certain actions as right and others as wrong. There is not a person alive who always does what he or she thinks is right, never mind what God thinks is right. We constantly condemn ourselves for digressing from our own standards of behavior. When we have a case of progressive spiritual blindness, those standards cease to mean anything. This is what has happened to our society since World War II and what began the decline of faithfulness we've seen in seminaries and churches.

Paul gives a graphic example of turning away in Romans 1:18–21:

> The wrath of God is being revealed from heaven against all the godlessness and wickedness of men who suppress the truth by their wickedness, since what may be known about God is plain to them, because God has made it plain to them. For since the creation of the world God's invisible qualities—his eternal power and divine nature—have been clearly seen, being understood from what has been made, so that men are without excuse.
>
> For although they knew God, they neither glorified him as God nor gave thanks to him, but their thinking became futile and their foolish hearts were darkened.

By suppressing the truth, they turned away from God, neither glorifying nor thanking Him. Their hearts were darkened. Their thinking became futile, and Paul says they are without excuse. While modern-day Pharisees may be a prime example of those who have turned away, the warning is also for us.

The first result of turning from something we know to be right or true is intellectual confusion. This leads to actions that are misinformed, and Paul has some strong words for that: "Although they claimed to be wise, they became fools" (verse 22). What was foolish? Their actions were a form of idolatry; they "exchanged the glory of the immortal God for images made to look like mortal man and birds and animals and reptiles" (verse 23).

Idolatry isn't limited to statuary. People practice idolatry whenever they substitute something else for God as their ultimate concern. That's what happens when we turn to our own ways of rebellion or unbelief; it's an easy downhill slide all the way. "Therefore God gave them over in the sinful desires of their hearts to sexual impurity for the degrading of their bodies with one another. They exchanged the truth of God for a lie, and worshiped and served created things rather than the Creator—who is forever praised. Amen" (verses 24–25).

Have you followed the progression so far? Disobedience begins with unbelief, then justification of behavior, turning away, talking ourselves into things we know to be false. Little by little, as we learn to live with our evil ways, we have substituted something else for the true God as the object of our first loyalty and affection. When we keep God from His proper place, when we refuse to recognize that we are created in His image and that our bodies were made for Him, our behavior becomes immoral.

Bitterness

> Anyone who claims to be in the light but hates his brother is still in the darkness. Whoever loves his brother lives in the light, and there is nothing in him to make him stumble. But whoever hates his brother is in the darkness and walks around in the darkness; he does not know where he is going, because the darkness has blinded him.   1 John 2:9–11

This is a very down-to-earth reality that we often avoid. If I were God, I would not have done as He did, connecting love for Him with love for others. It would have been sufficient to love God with all one's heart, soul, and mind.

Many would agree with me, and many more act as if that were the case! Jesus, however, said we must love God *and* love our neighbor. The degree to which we do not do this is the degree to which we walk in the darkness of bitterness.

It is interesting to note that the theological exchanges among the various schools of thought in the Church have been publicly devoid of any love. One side cites Scripture, tradition, and reason. The other seeks to give experience equal, if not superior, weight. There have been acrimonious exchanges, with epithets hurled back and forth; in fact, new terms have been added to the ecclesiastical language.

First John is often used as a last defense, when the argument is clearly not being won by either side; for, in truth, we all lose when one is unwilling to see clearly. "Unloving!" someone shouts, and it's often true, as by then considerable ire has been produced. Both sides retreat. The discussion ends, and bitterness begins. Bitterness comes from an unloving attitude on either the giving or the receiving end. Look at 1 John 2:9–11 again, with a theological argument in mind.

Verse 9: "Anyone who claims to be in the light but hates his brother is still in the darkness." Orthodoxy is not enough; you can't produce faith without love, and real love is not possible without orthodoxy—"being in the light."

Verse 10: "Whoever loves his brother lives in the light, and there is nothing in him to make him stumble." *Living in the light* implies that the actions of the person's life under scrutiny would not be displeasing to the Lord. Believing *and* behaving are what make for real love.

Verse 11: "But whoever hates his brother is in the darkness and walks around in the darkness; he does not know where he is going, because the darkness has blinded him." The actions that lead to darkness are those not pleasing to God. Such actions don't seek change and repentance and light. People let the bitterness build up. They walk around in the darkness, justifying it, perhaps bringing others into the darkness with them. John says that converting people to darkness is actually hating, not loving, those who are led away from the light. It is far more loving to set people back on the right path. The path to darkness is dangerous, and neither the leader nor the follower knows where it leads, because they both have been blinded by their refusal to see.

It is human and understandable to feel resentment, to feel less than loving all the time. Not repenting of resentment, nursing the unloving response until it becomes full-blown bitterness, is another matter. Harboring bitterness and resentment is putting on a spiritual blindfold. Trying to see God this way is like trying to watch television wearing distorting eyeglasses. We'll find our picture of God is slightly out of focus; the delineation is fuzzy; the colors are distorted; we don't get much from it.

Understand this: It is on the receiving end of God's love that the change has taken place. The transmission is as clear as ever. Just because people can't see something physically does not mean that it has not happened. It is the same spiritually: God is still actively loving and renewing His people—those who will remove their bitter eyeglasses, even blindfolds, and have eyes to see clearly.

When the apostle Paul (formerly Saul of Tarsus) was knocked off his horse on the road to Damascus and confronted by a light brighter than the sun, he was told by the living Lord Jesus:

> "Now get up and stand on your feet. I have appeared to you to appoint you as a servant and as a witness of what you have seen of me and what I will show you. I will rescue you from your own people and from the Gentiles. I am sending you to open their eyes and turn them from darkness to light, and from the power of Satan to God, so that they may receive forgiveness of sins and a place among those who are sanctified by faith in me."
>
> Acts 26:16–18

God, who was sending Paul to combat spiritual blindness, made him experience physical blindness for a brief time in preparation.

Dealing with Spiritual Blindness

Jesus' instruction to the man born blind (John 9) gives insight into how we can combat spiritual blindness. Jesus did not say to him, *"If* you wash in the pool of Siloam, you will be healed." There wasn't a promise. He simply said, *"Go."* Jesus could have opened the man's eyes right then and there without touching him. Why did He have him go through a complicated procedure? The answer is obedience. Jesus requires obedience as a key to receiving our spiritual sight. Jesus didn't argue or explain. He simply said, *"Go."*

The man could have argued, "Why did You put mud on my eyes?" He could have questioned, "Will I actually be healed if I do this?" He could have rebelled, "I don't want to go to the pool. Heal me here!" But he didn't. He obeyed and was healed.

God often interposes steps between affliction and healing, the reason for which may be impossible for us to figure out in advance. Yet our response to these steps makes all the difference between spiritual blindness and vision.

Such obedience was required of Naaman, the Syrian commander in the Old Testament. Naaman was a high man in government; he was also a leper. A Jewish girl in his household (who might have hated her master because he was an unclean foreigner), feeling compassion and love for him, told him about the healing prophet Elisha. Out of desperation Naaman went to see Elisha, who relayed instructions through his servant to "go, wash yourself seven times in the Jordan" (2 Kings 5:10).

The Syrian commander was appalled. Not only had Elisha not received him personally, he had given him the demeaning task of bathing in the Jordan River, which is not more than a muddy trickle in places. Naaman turned away at first, but when his servants urged him to obey the prophet's simple instructions, he went down to the river.

Can't you just see him walking to the edge of the water, filled with humiliation and disgust? Imagine him wading into it, dipping once, and looking at his skin to see if there was any change. Then dipping twice, three times. Still no change. *This is outrageous*, he might have said to himself. *Well*, he might have thought, *the prophet did say seven times.* He was already wet, so he dipped the fourth, fifth, and sixth times. When he came up from the seventh dip, much to his amazement, his skin was as pink and smooth as a child's.

Now, Elisha could have said, "Be healed!" and have been done with it, but God put steps of obedience between the affliction and the cure. Today He might direct us to follow the counsel of a doctor, since God heals through medication as well as by miracle. In terms of the healing of our minds or our emotions, He might direct us to a compassionate counselor whose instructions we must follow. In every case, our response to His instructions will govern our progress toward spiritual sight or blindness. He wants us to trust Him!

In the Faith Alive movement in the Episcopal Church, the children's coordinators lead a "faith walk" exercise. Children pair off, and one is blindfolded. The other is told to guide the partner around the building or the yard. The guiding partner gives clues, such as "Step down now"; "We're going to turn left." It's amazing to watch how quickly these bundles of energy turn into cautious, careful guides. Each child takes a turn being responsible for the other and also trusting his or her safety to someone else. They are then told that trusting God is like going on a faith walk with God as the Guide who can see where we are going; He guides us carefully every step of the way.

Summary

Just as having a periodic eye examination is important in the physical realm, examining our spiritual vision is crucial. The psalmist wrote: "The law of the Lord is perfect, reviving the soul. The statutes of the Lord are trustworthy, making wise the simple. The precepts of the Lord are right, giving joy to the heart. The commands of the Lord are radiant, giving light to the eyes" (Psalm 19:7–8).

As we come to know God more intimately, learning His will, His commands, learning to obey them and trust Him, loving who He is as well as what He does, our spiritual eyes will be opened, and He will fill our lives with light.

Warm-Up Exercises

1. In what area of your life do you feel a need for spiritual light?

2. Are there other people involved? That is, do you need to forgive or be forgiven?

3. What corrective action do you need to take to allow the laser beam of the Holy Spirit to open your eyes again?

4. How is your "faith walk"? Do you need to trust God more?

Stretching

Memorize Psalm 119:18 and pray it often: "Open my eyes that I may see wonderful things in your law."

3

Ears to Hear

Our ears are interesting and complicated parts of our bodies. What we interpret as hearing is actually a response to sound waves that move through the air. The sound waves are translated into coded nerve impulses, which are transformed into vibrations of the eardrum; the movements of the drum are changed into vibrations of three small bones that comprise the middle ear, which are in turn converted into movements of fluid in the ear, which exert tension on the hair cells of the organ of Corti, and finally generate nerve impulses in the auditory nerve. A miraculous transformation! The intricacy of the ear's design is certainly wonderful evidence for our Creator. The point is, interference with the hearing process at any point along the way can result in a loss of hearing and ultimately deafness.

Our means of spiritual hearing is every bit as delicate as the physical system. God's dealings with human beings require a response to the many ways He communicates with us. Most often, He communicates in ways other than through our physical auditory system. When you hear people say, "The Lord told me," it is not likely that they have heard an audible voice. God speaks to us most often through his written Word, through others, and through inspiration—an inner voice of the indwelling Holy Spirit. But the fact is, God does speak to His people!

Revelation and Response

God is not the product of our wishful thinking or overzealous imagination. We have not learned about Him through individual or corporate observation. God has addressed us out of the silence of eternity. He is not a mute deity out there somewhere, not an abstract philosophical principle or a cosmic ooze in the vastness of the universe. God is living; He communicates with His creation and expects communication in return. Theologians call this "revelation." Hebrews 1 says, "In the past God spoke to our forefathers through the prophets at many times and in various ways, but in these last days he has spoken to us by his Son, whom he appointed heir of all things, and through whom he made the universe" (verses 1–2).

The revelation of God was first to our forefathers, then through the prophets, and ultimately through Jesus, who in turn sent the Holy Spirit to remain with us, to be the means of communication between God and His people.

In the book of the prophet Isaiah, God issues a summons: "Come, all you who are thirsty, come to the waters; and you who have no money, come, buy and eat! . . . Why spend money on what is not bread, and your labor on what does not satisfy? Listen, listen to me, and eat what is good, and your soul will delight in the richest of fare. Give ear and come to me; hear me, that your soul may live" (Isaiah 55:1–3a).

This passage implies that just as surely as God speaks, we can choose our response. There are different levels of listening: listening, selective listening, and active listening.

Listening pertains to the hearing one does when the heart is not really in it—like a boy stuck in a classroom when a bright spring day beckons him outdoors. The teacher's lessons buzz around him, but he understands very little and retains less.

Selective listening is the kind of listening you most often get from teenagers. They retain what they want to hear and ignore the rest, although what they ignore may be precisely what they need to have communicated to them.

Active listening is practiced by people who are interested in each other. There is total involvement and a high degree of retention; years later some people can recall conversations verbatim. What God desires from His people is active listening, and He gives us a promise: "Your soul will delight in the richest of fare. . . . hear me, that your soul may live.".

Prophecy: Listening to Proclaim

There are two sides to this issue of God's revelation to us: God's Word must be proclaimed and God's Word must be heard and obeyed. Both require the use of our ears—physical or spiritual.

To proclaim God's Word, one first has to hear it. One of the primary individuals responsible for hearing God's Word is, in biblical language, the prophet. Don't imagine a man with a long, flowing beard who walks around predicting the future. A prophet is more distinguished by *forth-telling* than foretelling. Prophecy is speaking the Word of God with conviction

A good way to get a handle on the concept of prophet (and, therefore, on the concept of spiritual hearing) is to recall the story of Moses and Aaron in Exodus 4. God called Moses to return to Egypt and lead the Israelites out of bondage, and Moses' response was less than enthusiastic: "Moses said to the Lord, 'O Lord, I have never been eloquent, neither in the past nor since you have spoken to your servant. I am slow of speech and tongue' " (verse 10).

I love the exchange that follows. God assures Moses that He made Moses' mouth and will enable him, but Moses pleads with the Almighty to send someone else. We may never have heard of Moses!

> Then the Lord's anger burned against Moses and he said, "What about your brother, Aaron the Levite? I know he can speak well. He is already on his way to meet you, and his heart will be glad when he sees you. You shall speak to him and put words in his mouth; I will help both of you speak and will teach you what to do. He will speak to the people for you, and it will be as if he were your mouth and as if you were God to him."   verses 14–16

God did not originally intend to use Aaron as a spokesman for Moses. Aaron is later called a prophet—a spokesman. Because Moses did not believe God would help him to speak and teach him what to say, God had to put a secondary plan into motion. As we read the story, we find it didn't work out very well.

Understanding the relationship between Moses and Aaron, we understand the function of prophet—and why spiritual ears are necessary for the proclamation of God's Word. The message does not originate with the prophet; he has to hear his message from another source. Aaron didn't prepare a speech; he listened to his brother and acted as his mouthpiece—God helping them both. God spoke to Moses. Moses needed help speaking to Aaron, who needed help hearing. Aaron needed help speaking to the people, who needed help hearing. A prophet, then, is a person who, with God's help, hears God's Word and relays it to others. The great prophets of Israel often prefaced their remarks by saying, "The word of the Lord came to me, saying . . ." and they then proceeded to speak in the first person, as though God Himself were speaking.

God didn't have to do it that way, of course. He could have spoken directly to the human race. I think, if I were God, I would have preferred it that way. (Can you imagine it? "Attention, world! I am the Lord your God!" spoken with a voice thundering from the control room of the universe.) But God chose to speak through human agents through the ages and continues to do so to the present day. We are encouraged to "eagerly desire" the prophetic gift, one of the spiritual gifts listed in 1 Corinthians 12–14.

Not every prophet speaks from God. The difference lies in the quality of the prophet's hearing ability. A prophet is a person under orders, delivering the message God has spoken. If at a particular point God has not spoken, the prophet should have nothing to say. Yet, as we read in Scripture, many have spoken out in their own authority:

> "This is what the Lord Almighty says: 'Do not listen to what the prophets are prophesying to you; they fill you with false hopes. They speak visions from their own minds, not from the mouth of the Lord. . . . But which of them has stood in the council of the Lord to see or to hear his word? Who has listened and heard his word?' "
>
> Jeremiah 23:16, 18

A true prophet stands in the presence of God, hears His Word, and receives His help to deliver it. A false prophet, perhaps due to selective spiritual hearing, delivers visions of his or her own creation. A false prophet has not heard the Word of God and most likely has not spent time in His presence, as God does not speak to strangers. As a result of this ministry, hearers are misled.

The Lord had more to say to Jeremiah: "They keep saying to those who despise me, 'The Lord says: You will have peace.' And to all who follow the stubbornness of their hearts they say, 'No harm will come to you.' . . . But if they had stood in my council, they would have proclaimed my words to my people and would have turned them from their evil ways and from their evil deeds" (23:17, 22).

False teaching and preaching are prevalent today, in spite of a renewed emphasis on biblical values and teaching. In churches where no one's life is changed year after year, it may be that no one is standing in God's presence, hearing and seeking God's help in delivering the Word of God; there is no prophetic voice.

In some highly visible ecclesiastical circles today, some are claiming a "prophetic voice" and uttering things that go against God's Word. Be aware: Unless the spoken word attributed to God agrees with the written Word of God, the prophetic utterance is not of God. Not everyone who stands in a pulpit declares the Word of God. Not everyone who wears clerical garb and precedes his or her name with *Reverend* has stood in God's presence. Any person— whether Sunday school teacher, pastor or bishop, or spouse or friend giving advice—who ever delivers a message of his or her own origin undermines the Word of God and encourages rebellion against God. " 'I did not send these prophets, yet they have run with their message; I did not speak to them, yet they have prophesied. . . . I have heard what the prophets say who prophesy lies in my name. . . . They tell them and lead my people astray with their reckless lies, yet I did not send or appoint them. They do not benefit these people in the least,' declares the Lord" (Jeremiah 23:21, 25a, 32b).

Messages from the human mind cannot nourish the spirit. Many who come to church to receive the bread of life are instead given straw. "Let the prophet who has a dream tell his dream, but let the one who has my word speak it faithfully. For what has straw to do with grain?" (verse 28).

Through the prophet Isaiah, God offers a warning to those ministers not delivering His Word faithfully: "Hear, you deaf; look, you blind, and see! Who is blind but my servant, and deaf like the messenger I send? Who is blind like the one committed to me, blind like the servant of the Lord? You have seen many things, but have paid no attention; your ears are open, but you hear nothing" (Isaiah 42:18–20).

God holds His servants accountable. They are held

responsible for listening or not listening to Him. This was
not only true for Israel; it is true today for those at every
level of the Church. God expects the clergy to hear and to
deliver His Word, and nothing else. It is impossible to
keep a congregation alive without nourishment.

Listening to Hear and Respond

Spiritual hearing also involves hearing the Word of God
so we can respond to it. It's sad to say that even when
God's Word is faithfully preached, not all who physically
hear it are active listeners, involved in the message and
eager to learn from it. Some may receive it as a garden
receives the spring rain—absorbing it and growing as a
result; others let it run off the surface of their lives, like
rain on an asphalt driveway. Whenever I stand to speak,
I know that some of my listeners will receive nourishment,
and others will refuse it. My job is to stand in the council
of God and to seek His help in proclaiming His Word.

Like physical deafness, spiritual deafness can have many
causes. Some people refuse to believe. Others choose the
"salad bar" approach to faith. They take one part of God's
Word as truth and not another part. They select parts that
are most palatable to them and leave the rest. No growth
and nourishment come from such selective belief. The
whole counsel of God is required.

Turning our wills from God's plan and purpose will also
cause our spiritual deafness. It is the spiritual equivalent
of the kind of deafness Bill Cosby describes in young
children: When they turn their backs to you, they cannot
hear you. Sometimes the spiritual battles people face are
nothing more than contests of their wills against God's
will for them. Prolonged rebellion will harden hearts
toward God, and damage spiritual ears.

When God communicates, He desires three reactions:
active listening, faithful response, and obedience. The lack
of proper listening to God's Word is described in Ezekiel

33. I pray I will never hear these words applied to my congregation:

> "As for you, son of man, your countrymen are talking together about you by the walls and at the doors of the houses, saying to each other, 'Come and hear the message that has come from the Lord.' My people come to you, as they usually do, and sit before you to listen to your words, but they do not put them into practice. With their mouths they express devotion, but their hearts are greedy for unjust gain. Indeed, to them you are nothing more than one who sings love songs with a beautiful voice and plays an instrument well, for they hear your words but do not put them into practice."   verses 30–32

Do people come to church to worship God and listen actively to His Word? Do they come to be entertained with music and special effects? We would do well to follow an admonition of Solomon: "Guard your steps when you go to the house of God. Go near to listen rather than to offer the sacrifice of fools, who do not know that they do wrong" (Ecclesiastes 5:1).

The work of the Holy Spirit must be active in the one who speaks and in the one who hears that spoken word. Both must be seeking to be fit for God's presence for spiritual hearing to occur.

The lack of faithful response to God's Word is shown in Hebrews 4:2: "For we also have had the gospel preached to us, just as they did; but the message they heard was of no value to them, because those who heard did not combine it with faith."

We can listen to God's Word and not hear it unless we combine it with faith. Jesus Himself, completely yielded to the Father and filled with the Holy Spirit, could do nothing in places such as Nazareth because of the unbelief of the people. On the other hand, in an atmosphere of faith He was free to work and miracles abounded.

It's not enough just to hear and respond. If the Word of

God stops there, with your rejoicing in your heart at the wonder of it all, it does not profit you or God. What you hear and what you believe must be translated into action. In the Ezekiel passage, the people heard but did not put God's Word into practice. James echoed that succinctly: "Do not merely listen to the word, and so deceive yourselves. Do what it says" (1:22).

Jesus illustrated this in the parable of the wise and foolish builders:

> "Therefore everyone who hears these words of mine and puts them into practice is like a wise man who built his house on the rock. The rain came down, the streams rose, and the winds blew and beat against that house; yet it did not fall, because it had its foundation on the rock. But everyone who hears these words of mine and does not put them into practice is like a foolish man who built his house on sand. The rain came down, the streams rose, and the winds blew and beat against that house, and it fell with a great crash."   Matthew 7:24–27

Practicing the Word of God gives strength to one's faith. It is an important part of the quest for spiritual fitness. As our physical ears affect the balance of our bodies, so our spiritual ears affect the balance of our spiritual lives. Without action, it is as if our inner ears are stopped and we can't walk straight. Without putting God's Word into action, we spiritually list to one side or dizzily wander around. It takes the living example of the Word of God to make it real to others, and as we live that example, we improve our spiritual fitness.

Summary

God chooses to speak His Word to the world through human beings—prophets who will declare His Word, not their own. Hearers need to be active listeners, with attentive minds, open hearts, and faithful responses. We are called to hear with our ears, that our minds may understand and our wills yield. What is the result? Actions exemplifying God's Word and corresponding to His purpose.

Warm-Up Exercises

1. How much time do you spend in the presence of the Lord?

2. What kind of listener are you to God's Word and His will?

3. What actions can you take to build up your spiritual fitness and that of others?

Stretching

Memorize Isaiah 55:3a. Note the four verbs in that passage: "Give ear and come to me; hear me, that your soul may live."

4

The Mouth

It is the greatest privilege of human beings to "join our voices with angels and archangels and with all the company of heaven" (as *The Book of Common Prayer* puts it) in praising the name of our God. One of the psalms of David demonstrates this activity in a remarkable way:

I will exalt you, my God the King;
  I will praise your name for ever and ever.
Every day I will praise you
  and extol your name for ever and ever. . . .
One generation will commend your works to another;
  they will tell of your mighty acts. . . .
They will tell of the power of your awesome works,
  and I will proclaim your great deeds.
They will celebrate your abundant goodness
  and joyfully sing of your righteousness.

Psalm 145:1–7

We can engage in no better exercise toward spiritual fitness than to exalt, praise, extol, commend, tell, proclaim, celebrate, and sing of the Lord. These are actions that flow from hearing and responding to the Word of God. And, as David's psalm says, we are to do it daily.

All of these exercises use our mouths. There are two parts of the mouth to which the Bible makes special reference: the lips and the tongue. These can participate in the worship of God and the commendation of God to others, or, if used carelessly, they can be instruments used to destroy other people and stop the love of Christ from growing in the unbeliever.

The right use of the mouth is an important part of physical fitness. "A moment on the lips, forever on the hips" is a popular phrase for dieters. Satisfying the desires of our taste buds for sweets and calorie-laden foods will work against the goals we have set. So it is spiritually—but it's not what goes into our mouths so much as what comes out through our speech that will deter our spiritual fitness.

Praise

We generally assume that we understand praise. Yet many misunderstand the motivation behind it. Is the God we worship an egomaniac who sits on a throne demanding to be told over and over how wonderful He is? Do we praise Him as we might an earthly ruler whose fragile ego requires it? Is praise a form of flattery?

I would rather have you think of praise to God as the overflow of a loving, grateful heart—one that enjoys Him and enjoys expressing that love. It is a reflection of a close relationship. No one needs to encourage a courting couple to praise each other or to extol the loved one's virtues to anyone who will listen!

In the Westminster Catechism, one question asks: "What is man's purpose on earth?" I love the response: "To glorify God and enjoy Him forever." The two are inseparable; we praise Him because we enjoy Him.

Praise is awkward for many church people. I suspect the reason is that they really don't enjoy the Lord. They may fear and respect Him, but they hold Him at arm's length. If the enjoyment of God is missing from their hearts, the praise of God is absent from their lips.

This may explain why praise in church is often dreary and unnatural. For instance, in the Episcopal service of Morning Prayer, the priest says, "Lord, open our lips,"

and the people respond, "And our mouth shall proclaim
your praise." They don't realize that they can open their
own mouths of praise. Or in a service of holy Communion, a poker-faced minister may intone, "The Lord is
risen." The people may mumble, "He is risen indeed,"
expressing no joy at all. It is not God's desire for His
people to meander perfunctorily through the Doxology:

> Praise God from whom all blessings flow,
> Praise Him, all creatures here below!
> Praise Him above, ye heavenly host,
> Praise Father, Son, and Holy Ghost!

The rafters should ring with those words!

Intimacy with God

God delights in His people, though I cannot imagine
why. What's more, He invites us to delight in Him. At our
church we sing a little song that declares our love and
praise for God. Then one line says, "Take joy, my King, in
what You hear." That idea is totally incomprehensible to
many Christians! They cannot grasp that their songs and
love for God would fill Him with delight, yet it is true.

God desires an intimate relationship with His people.
Scripture describes it in terms of marriage. "Your Maker is
your husband," declares Isaiah (54:5). Jesus is referred to
as the Bridegroom and the Church as His Bride. No other
image can quite capture the intensity of God's love for us
or the loving abandon with which He wants us to respond.
Nothing hidden, nothing held back—totally and completely at one with Him. Such a deep love produces praise
that is not the mere mouthing of words.

If we enjoy our relationship with God, we will speak of
Him to others. If we do not talk about Him, we probably
do not cherish Him deeply in our hearts. Personality
differences notwithstanding, if we are full of the life of

God, it will spill over into our conversations. If Jesus is the Lord of our lives, we will talk about Him. Many people have told me that their faith is a private thing to them. "Being a Christian is more than giving a verbal witness," they protest. "I want to witness with my life." The fact is, unless we are willing to attribute the way we live to the grace of God, few others will.

A hard-living young man of my acquaintance was converted at a church meeting in Maine. He went to work the following summer at a backwoods logging camp. His pastor, concerned that he would backslide in such a rough environment, asked him at the end of the summer how he had done as a new Christian. "Just fine," he replied. "Nobody even knew!"

Jesus has not called us all to be preachers, but He has called us all to be witnesses. We are to tell what we have experienced. If we love Him, we will want to obey Him; we will speak out for Him. This is the right use of the lips and tongue for our spiritual fitness.

Mouth Misuse

But we can also misuse our mouths so as to work against our quest for spiritual fitness. James spoke of this: "We all stumble in many ways. If anyone is never at fault in what he says, he is a perfect man, able to keep his whole body in check. . . . The tongue also is a fire, a world of evil among the parts of the body. It corrupts the whole person, sets the whole course of his life on fire, and is itself set on fire by hell" (3:2, 6).

Gossip, lies, and swearing will do incredible damage to the cause of Christ. James continued, "With the tongue we praise our Lord and Father, and with it we curse men, who have been made in God's likeness. Out of the same mouth come praise and cursing. My brothers, this should not be" (verses 9–10). Instead of using our mouths to talk about God to others, we talk about others to others and

actually defame those made in God's image. The tongue
has little physical strength, but it wields a great influence.
Its strength is disproportionate to its size.

Have you ever been victimized by someone else's
words? Have you been the subject of slander or gossip?
What about a lie? Oliver Wendell Holmes wrote, "Sin has
many tools, but a lie is a handle that fits them all." Has
anyone ever told a lie or a half-truth about you? Have you
ever had to straighten out a perception about yourself that
started with a misused mouth? And what about your own
actions—perhaps a casual remark you never should have
made, or an overstatement of a point that triggered a
seemingly endless string of pain? The tongue's poison
destroys like acid.

Swearing, like gossip and lying, can do great damage.
The Lord Jesus emphasized the connection between the
root and the fruit, between what is spoken and what it
reveals about the person:

> "Make a tree good and its fruit will be good, or make a
> tree bad and its fruit will be bad, for a tree is recognized by
> its fruit. You brood of vipers, how can you who are evil say
> anything good? For out of the overflow of the heart the
> mouth speaks. The good man brings good things out of the
> good stored up in him, and the evil man brings evil things
> out of the evil stored up in him. But I tell you that men will
> have to give account on the day of judgment for every
> careless word they have spoken. For by your words you
> will be acquitted, and by your words you will be con-
> demned."   Matthew 12:33–37

Hear this: Consistency counts! The mouth that pro-
claims the praise of the Lord in church on Sunday and
swears at the office on Monday condemns itself. Behavior
like this has caused many over the years to agree with
Nietzsche who said, "The last Christian died on the
cross." Nobody will believe the witness of a person's
actions if that person's speech contradicts them, no matter

how faithful he or she is in church participation or service. Jesus said that what a person utters originates in the heart. What tragic contradictions must reside in the heart of one who will praise God one minute and then moments later turn around and gossip about one He has made—or will sing to God in a service and moments later tell a lie to someone in the congregation?

A mouth fit for God's presence is what we are aiming for. Before you speak to another, ask yourself, "What would I say if God were listening?" because He is.

Summary

There are many Scriptures that speak of the importance of the right use of the tongue. Let me summarize with just four of them.

"The tongue of the righteous is choice silver, but the heart of the wicked is of little value" (Proverbs 10:20).

"Reckless words pierce like a sword, but the tongue of the wise brings healing" (Proverbs 12:18).

"The tongue that brings healing is a tree of life, but a deceitful tongue crushes the spirit" (Proverbs 15:4).

"Through Jesus, therefore, let us continually offer to God a sacrifice of praise—the fruit of lips that confess his name" (Hebrews 13:15).

How can we use our mouths to build spiritual fitness? By using our lips and tongue to offer praise and faithful, consistent witness to our God.

Warm-Up Exercises

1. How comfortable are you in giving praise to God?

2. How can you witness to His life within you?

3. What do you need to do to enhance your love for Jesus so that praise and witness will overflow?

4. Is gossip, lying, or swearing a problem for you? As either a victim or a practitioner, take time to forgive and be forgiven.

Stretching

Memorize Proverbs 15:4 as a guide for your spiritual fitness: "The tongue that brings healing is a tree of life, but a deceitful tongue crushes the spirit."

5

The Face

Perhaps no part of the physical body gets as much attention as the face. Songs and sonnets have been written about faces that have captured someone's imagination or adoration. But there's a flip side: Men and women spend millions of dollars every year trying to improve on the face God has given them. Facial massages, cosmetics and cosmetic surgery, creams and cleansers, skin bronzers and bleaches—all have one purpose: to make the faces that we show to the world more acceptable.

Faces tell much about us. A face is the most distinctive part of a body, as the eyes, nose, mouth, and chin differ in each person. Our features give a hint of our ethnic origin, the mood we are in, even the state of our physical health—skin flushed or pale, dry or damp, drawn or puffy.

We seldom realize that our faces can reflect the glory of God. Yet the Old Testament leader Moses exemplified this truth: A person's face can make the indwelling presence of God visible to others.

Moses had no idea that God would call him to lead the Israelites out of Egyptian bondage. At the time of Moses' birth, the Jews were not in favor with the Pharaoh. Since the children of Israel had multiplied in number, their Egyptian overlords were concerned that, in case of foreign invasion, the Hebrew slaves might help the enemy. To prevent that, Pharaoh ordered that all Jewish boys be killed at birth.

To save her baby, Moses' mother hid him by setting him afloat on the Nile River in a little basket. While bathing, the Pharaoh's daughter found him and raised him as her own son; she even hired Moses' mother to become his nursemaid. Though Moses grew up as an Egyptian, with an Egyptian education, his mother never let him forget he was a descendant of Israel; he had a covenantal relationship with the one true God.

Moses lived in Egypt for forty years. When he came upon an Egyptian soldier mercilessly beating a Hebrew slave, Moses killed the soldier. Fearing for his life, he fled to the wilderness, where he lived for another forty years, tending the flocks of his father-in-law, Jethro.

Both his Egyptian court life and his shepherding were preparation for the task God had chosen for Moses—to lead God's people out of Egypt and through the wilderness to the Promised Land. Moses, schooled in the ways of the Egyptians and familiar with the wilderness, knew every oasis and shelf of rock in the Sinai. He had been prepared through the seemingly ordinary circumstances of his life for this particular leadership. Take a message from that: If nothing dramatic is happening in your life, don't assume that God is passing you by! The time may yet come when all of your abilities and experiences will be needed to do a mighty work for God.

In Scripture accounts of three different encounters between Moses and God, Moses' face revealed the progression of his relationship with God—his spiritual fitness to be in God's presence.

Hiding Your Face

In his first encounter with God, Moses' attention was caught by a bush, burning but not consumed by the fire.

> When the Lord saw that he had gone over to look, God called to him from within the bush, "Moses, Moses!"
>
> And Moses said, "Here I am."
>
> "Do not come any closer," God said. "Take off your sandals, for the place where you are standing is holy ground." Then he said, "I am the God of your father, the God of Abraham, the God of Isaac and the God of Jacob." At this, Moses hid his face, because he was afraid to look at God.
>
> Exodus 3:4–6

Why did Moses hide his face in fear? Understand what God was telling Moses about Himself. Centuries before, God had called Abraham to father a race of people with whom God would have a covenantal relationship. He had renewed the covenant with Abraham's son Isaac, and with Isaac's son Jacob. The Hebrews whom God was now calling Moses to deliver were all descendants of Abraham. God was saying, "I want you to know whom you're dealing with, Moses. I am the One who called Abraham out of Ur and led him across traceless wastes to the land of promise. I am the One who, in Abraham's and Sarah's old age, gave them a son named Isaac. I am the One who renewed My covenant with Isaac, and with Isaac's son Jacob, whose twelve sons fathered the twelve tribes of Israel. Be aware, Moses, of who I am."

Moses, confronted with this awesome review of the mighty acts of God and knowing of God's holiness, hid his face in fear.

God still reveals Himself in mighty acts today. Before we can begin to experience God in our lives, we must learn about what He has done in the lives of others, either in Bible times, throughout history, or more recently. We then will understand that God is still around, still active, and that He still cares for His people. Faced with that realization, we can either hide in fear or turn to Him in worship.

Face to Face

Moses did not remain fearful of an encounter with God.
Later encounters as Moses was leading the Israelites
toward the Promised Land show that Moses and God's
relationship grew direct and intimate.

> Now Moses used to take a tent and pitch it outside the
> camp some distance away, calling it the "tent of meeting."
> Anyone inquiring of the Lord would go to the tent of
> meeting outside the camp. . . . As Moses went into the
> tent, the pillar of cloud would come down and stay at the
> entrance, while the Lord spoke with Moses. . . . The Lord
> would speak to Moses face to face, as a man speaks with
> his friend.   Exodus 33:7, 9, 11b

Theologians call this encounter a theophany—a manifestation of God. Moses was in the presence of the *shekinah*
glory—a shining light that symbolizes God's presence.
People who have never read the Bible may know about the
shekinah glory from the movie *Raiders of the Lost Ark*. In that
movie it is portrayed as swirling, brilliant light that none
could look upon without destruction. Not so with Moses;
he could stand face to face with the *shekinah* glory of God.
Moses knew God as *friend*, and God longs for the same
intimacy with us.

Transformed Face

When Moses spent forty days on Mount Sinai and
received the Law, his face was radically transformed.

> When Aaron and all the Israelites saw Moses, his face
> was radiant, and they were afraid to come near him. . . .
> When Moses finished speaking to them, he put a veil
> over his face. But whenever he entered the Lord's presence
> to speak with him, he removed the veil until he came out.
> And when he came out and told the Israelites what he had

been commanded, they saw that his face was radiant.
Then Moses would put the veil back over his face until he
went in to speak with the Lord.   Exodus 34:30, 33–35

Moses' countenance was transformed because he had
spent time with God. When we turn our faces toward
God, they will inevitably reflect some of His glory. Jesus
referred to this in His high priestly prayer: "I have given
them the glory that you gave me" (John 17:22a). You
might think of this in terms of the moon, which reflects
the light of the sun. The moon has no light of its own, but
the light it reflects shines brightly. Our faces will shine
with the reflection of the glory of God if we spend time in
His presence.

The apostle Paul commented on the change in Moses'
face, and used it as a contrast between the Law of Moses
and the Holy Spirit: "Now if the ministry that brought
death, which was engraved in letters on stone, came with
glory, so that the Israelites could not look steadily at the
face of Moses because of its glory, fading though it was,
will not the ministry of the Spirit be even more glorious?"
(2 Corinthians 3:7–8).

How wonderful it must have been to stand at the foot of
Mount Sinai, to see the fire and feel the tremors in the
ground caused by the presence of the power of the Lord
God! It must have been awe-inspiring to see Moses
descend from the mountain, his face aglow with God's
glory. But, Paul says, if you think that was splendid, "you
ain't seen nothin' yet!" The ministry of the Holy Spirit
brings greater splendor. "If the ministry that condemns
men is glorious, how much more glorious is the ministry
that brings righteousness! For what was glorious has no
glory now in comparison with the surpassing glory. And
if what was fading away came with glory, how much
greater is the glory of that which lasts!" (2 Corinthians
3:9–11).

How does it work? The Law of Moses condemned

sinners. Jesus was sent to do the work of atonement for sins. This He did on the cross; in His death and resurrection all sins are forgiven. After He ascended to the Father, He sent the Holy Spirit to continue His work in God's people.

The Spirit of God begins to work obedience from the inside out. This obedience is "deeper" than was possible under the Law, which called for simple adherence to a set of rules. We are transformed by the Spirit from the inside out; this is no skin-deep beauty, and it lasts.

> Therefore, since we have such a hope, we are very bold. We are not like Moses, who would put a veil over his face to keep the Israelites from gazing at it while the radiance was fading away. But their minds were made dull, for to this day the same veil remains when the old covenant is read. It has not been removed, because only in Christ is it taken away.   2 Corinthians 3:12–14

God has established laws in the universe that will result in inevitable consequences if violated. If I jump from the top of one of the towers of the World Trade Center, I will be smashed on the sidewalk. God did not cause my fate; I did, in violating the natural law of gravity. Similarly, God has established a moral law in the universe that if violated has inevitable results. Those results are the darkening of my mind, the hardening of my heart, and the diminution of my responsiveness toward Him. And it will show on my face.

Have you ever met someone who was, at first glance, physically beautiful, but whose soul was so dark that your whole perception of his or her appearance changed? Or have you met someone whose face at first seemed ordinary, but when speaking of Christ that face became so transformed that you were transfixed with its attractiveness?

Here's why: "Whenever anyone turns to the Lord, the

veil is taken away. Now the Lord is the Spirit, and where the Spirit of the Lord is, there is freedom. And we, who with unveiled faces all reflect the Lord's glory, are being transformed into his likeness with ever-increasing glory, which comes from the Lord, who is the Spirit" (2 Corinthians 3:16–18). As representatives of our Father God, we are glory people. If we continually turn our faces toward His, He will pass His glory on to us. It is God's beauty plan to transform us from the inside out, little by little, by the indwelling of the Holy Spirit.

Unlike the beauty treatments of the world, we are not self-conscious about this transformation. It is our God-consciousness that works the change. We may never even be aware that we are reflecting God's radiance, but others will discern in us a glow that originates somewhere other than the world around us. We have a face fit for God's presence.

Summary

Behold the glory of God without fear. Let Him transform you from one degree of glory to another. Become a brilliant reflector of the light of the glory of God. People will be drawn to the light and to the One who gives it.

No greater blessing can be given than that found in Numbers 6:25: "The Lord make his face shine upon you."

Warm-Up Exercises

1. What do you like about the physical face God gave you? What would you like to change about it?

2. What would your reaction be to seeing God face to face?

3. Turn to the Lord and allow Him to start you on His

beauty plan—transforming you from the inside out into
His glory.

Stretching

Memorize 2 Corinthians 3:16–18 and look for signs of
the transformation: "But whenever anyone turns to the
Lord, the veil is taken away. Now the Lord is the Spirit,
and where the Spirit of the Lord is, there is freedom. And
we, who with unveiled faces all reflect the Lord's glory,
are being transformed into his likeness with ever-
increasing glory, which comes from the Lord, who is the
Spirit."

6

The Hands

In the process of all the oohing and aahing that takes place when a baby is first examined by relatives and friends, you will inevitably hear this comment: "Look at those hands! Did you ever see anything so perfect, so beautiful?"

Our hands are wonderfully made, especially created to grasp things—to hold, to touch, and to feel. The human hand contains at least four types of nerve endings that make the fingers and thumbs highly sensitive and responsive. Blind persons rely on their sense of touch when reading Braille; they run their fingertips over the raised dots. Our hands are extremely flexible, with twenty-seven bones and twenty muscles to enable movement. Evolutionists say that humanity's progress would have been hampered if we did not have opposable thumbs—thumbs that can be moved against our fingers. Perhaps realizing that, artist Auguste Rodin sculpted a graceful pair of hands and titled the piece "The Secret."

Our hands help us communicate with one another. Think about sign language and various hand gestures that are common to everyday conversation. You see the thumbs-up sign for victory, the clenched fist for rebellion, the wave of greeting. People in many cultures extend and shake right hands by way of introduction.

There are four ways the Bible talks about hands as part of our spiritual fitness. Clean hands are symbolic of holiness. The laying on of hands is the means of conferring God's grace in many aspects of ministry. The work of our hands in making a living is a gift from God. We lift our hands to God in worship.

Clean Hands, Pure Heart

Clean hands symbolize purity, the holiness without which we are not fit for God's presence. David asked two penetrating questions in Psalm 24:3–4: "Who may ascend the hill of the Lord? Who may stand in his holy place? He who has clean hands and a pure heart, who does not lift up his soul to an idol or swear by what is false." In Psalm 26:6–7 he said, "I wash my hands in innocence, and go about your altar, O Lord, proclaiming aloud your praise and telling of all your wonderful deeds."

Clean hands were required when one came into God's presence. The washing of hands was symbolic of the washing away of sins one had committed. You will still find ritual washing in Jewish tradition.

We are dealing with a holy God. Once we acknowledge that our hands are not clean and that our sins prevent us from being in God's presence, we have only two choices. We can trust in Jesus, recognizing His death as the bridge across the gulf of sin that separates us from God, or we can trust in our own personal virtue, hoping that we will somehow have the righteousness it takes to make us fit for God's presence.

Millions of people take their chances with the latter approach. They see Christianity as a religion of good works. They try to be good, hoping they can be good enough. Even within the Church, many understand their salvation as something to be won by prayers, sacrifice, or acts of generosity. The theory is that in the balance scales of life the good deeds will outweigh the bad ones; on that basis people hope to have a favorable reception by God.

But if that were the case, would we ever know where we stood from one day to the next? One day we'd be in, the next, out! One verse of Scripture blows the whole basis of that uncertain philosophy to bits. The prophet Isaiah wrote, "All of us have become like one who is unclean, and all our righteous acts are like filthy rags; we all shrivel up like a leaf, and like the wind our sins sweep us away" (64:6). All our *righteous* acts, the *best* we possibly can do, are detestable to God.

The Book of Common Prayer contains the Prayer of Humble Access, which includes a statement that prompts an exquisite sense of our unworthiness: "We do not presume to come to this thy Table, O merciful Lord, trusting in our own righteousness, but in thy manifold and great mercies. We are not worthy so much as to gather up the crumbs under thy Table. . . ." Our salvation is a gift, a gift of mercy. God owes us nothing. Our salvation is not a wage, something we earn. In order to appreciate the Gospel— the Good News—we first must hear the bad news: We cannot save ourselves.

Our hands are dirty. The best we can do is filthy in God's sight. Once we acknowledge that, we can trust in Christ to save us, to wash our hands clean, and give us His own spotless garments in which to stand before the Father.

In Jesus' parable about a wedding (Matthew 22:1–14) a man not wearing a wedding garment was thrown out by the master of the feast. That sounds strange to us until we understand that in that part of the world, even today, the host of a wedding party provided all of his guests with a wedding garment. When a guest arrived, his hands and feet were washed and the proper garment was slipped over his head. The man at the banquet without a garment had either refused it or entered illegitimately, and the feast was in danger of being defiled.

A person defiled with sin is not fit for God's presence. Paul wrote, "Clothe yourselves with the Lord Jesus Christ, and do not think about how to gratify the desires of the sinful nature" (Romans 13:14). With our hands washed in the blood of His sacrifice on the cross, with our spirits clothed in His righteousness and victory, we are fit for God's presence.

The Laying On of Hands

The laying on of hands is mentioned four ways in the Bible. Hands are laid on offerings to consecrate them to God and on people to set them apart for service to God. Hands are also laid on people to impart a blessing from God and to facilitate the means of God's healing grace.

Consecrating Offerings

The laying on of hands was first used as a means of consecrating offerings to the Lord. Throughout Leviticus we find the priests laying their hands on the various offerings of the people, praying over them, and consecrating them to God as an atonement for their sins. On the Day of Atonement, the high priest would lay hands on the scapegoat, conferring on it the sins of the people. The scapegoat was then led away, out of the people's sight—a graphic picture of Christ bearing our sins away from us.

Consecrating People

The laying on of hands in the consecration, or setting apart, of people for special, functional service before God is first mentioned when God instructed Moses to set apart the tribe of Levi to serve the Tabernacle in a nonpriestly capacity. God told Moses that the Levites must be cleansed before they could serve, harking back to the necessity of having clean hands to approach Him. Then He said, "You are to bring the Levites before the Lord, and the Israelites are to lay their hands on them. Aaron is to present the

Levites before the Lord as a wave offering from the Israelites, so that they may be ready to do the work of the Lord" (Numbers 8:10–11).

The Levites were made ready to do the Lord's work as the Israelites laid hands on them, presenting them before the Lord. This is the concept behind what we call "ordination." The whole nation of Israel was responsible for the commissioning of the Levites to their special service or function; today a congregation sponsors a candidate for ordination.

When Moses realized that his time on earth was coming to a close and he could no longer lead the children of Israel, God said to him: "Take Joshua son of Nun, a man in whom is the spirit, and lay your hand on him. Have him stand before Eleazar the priest and the entire assembly and commission him in their presence" (Numbers 27:18–19). God had chosen Joshua for his right spirit, and God was setting down the specifications for an ordination ceremony in which a leader would be set apart. Because the people could watch Moses commission his successor, Joshua, they would accept his leadership after Moses' death. The laying on of Moses' hands was the means God used to authorize Joshua's ministry.

Centuries later, in the early Church, the twelve apostles who served with a ministry of prayer and preaching acknowledged that certain widows were being neglected in the church's daily distribution of food. They instructed the body of disciples to select seven men to oversee this food distribution. "Brothers, choose seven men from among you who are known to be full of the Spirit and wisdom" (Acts 6:3a). The book of Acts further records that "They presented these men to the apostles, who prayed and laid their hands on them" (6:6).

Known to be full of the Spirit and of wisdom, the seven men were set apart for a specific function or task by prayer and the laying on of hands. These two acts have been part of every ordination in apostolic succession since then.

A second functional ordination within the Church is recorded several chapters later when Paul and Barnabas were commissioned for their first missionary journey by the believers at Antioch. The believers were fasting and praying and worshiping the Lord when the instructions came to send Paul and Barnabas out. "While they were worshiping the Lord and fasting, the Holy Spirit said, 'Set apart for me Barnabas and Saul [Paul] for the work to which I have called them.' So after they had fasted and prayed, they placed their hands on them and sent them off" (Acts 13:2–3). Today, prior to ordination, candidates retreat for a period of fasting and prayer, to make a complete confession and to worship the Lord.

A third example of functional ordination in the early Church involves Timothy, the young Greek Christian probably converted by Paul on that first missionary journey. In both New Testament letters bearing his name, Timothy was given fatherly advice by the aging apostle: "Do not neglect your gift, which was given you through a prophetic message when the body of elders laid their hands on you" (1 Timothy 4:14); "I remind you to fan into flame the gift of God, which is in you through the laying on of my hands" (2 Timothy 1:6).

At his ordination prophetic utterance and a specific manifestation of the Holy Spirit's gifts were received. Sad to say, that is no longer expected at ordination services. Paul later reminds Timothy of the importance of the laying on of hands and warns him not to do so hastily and not to share in the sins of others. Discerning a call to service was an important matter to be given long and careful thought in prayer, fasting, and worship. The wrong candidate would not minister to the glory of God.

Over the centuries, however, something tragic happened; the sense of God-ordained functional service degenerated into hierarchical ordination, with less and less caution being exercised as to the rightness of the spirit of the candidates for ordination. The church became another profession, like the law, the military, and other positions of visible leadership.

For centuries in Europe, the oldest son of a well-to-do family would inherit the estate and follow in his father's footsteps. The second son would become an officer in the military, and the third would become a priest. Families would offer sons to the Church to seek favors or to make up for some offense.

Influenced by the world's standards of achievement, people who had received the laying on of hands began to see themselves and be seen by others as being set *above* their fellow servants in the congregation. It was not intended to be that way. The laity are the people of God, those whom the ordained were set apart to serve.

Today, within the Episcopal Church, the laity are perceived as standing below the ecclesiastical ladder, which looks like this: On the first rung is the order of deacons, which means "those called to serve." Actually, no matter what other level the ordained clergy attain, they are always deacons, always called to serve. On the second rung stand the priests, some with lofty titles, such as dean or canon, denoting a specific function within their function. (A canon, I explain to my people, is a big shot.) Bishops are above them and archbishops stand in their lofty position at the top of the ladder. At each rung, hands are laid on the candidate to initiate him or her into the particular ministry.

Such a hierarchy underscores the almost universally accepted belief that the Church consists of two groups—the ministers who minister and the congregations who congregate. Such a view distorts the biblical understanding of ministry. The Bible provides a place for ordained ministry in the Body of Christ, but it also teaches that we have *all* been called to the priesthood. A sample from the Old Testament: "You will be for me a kingdom of priests and a holy nation" (Exodus 19:6a). An echo in the New Testament: "To him who loves us and has freed us from our sins by his blood, and has made us to be a kingdom and priests to serve his God and Father—to him be glory and power for ever and ever! Amen" (Revelation 1:5b–6).

If you are a Christian, Jesus has made you a priest. Never once, after Jesus instituted the New Covenant at the Last Supper, does Scripture use the word *priest* to refer to what you and I would call a clergyman. It applies first to Jesus Christ, the great High Priest who stands between us and God, and then to every person who has been freed from his or her sins.

We will never understand the biblical doctrine of ministry until we realize that Jesus never committed the task of spreading the Good News of His Kingdom to a cast of religious professionals. Nor does the New Testament anywhere espouse the tradition of a hierarchical priesthood. All believers are seen as priests, which is why our weekly church bulletin, after listing the clergy, adds: "Ministers: The entire congregation."

Ministry for All

As an ordained priest of the Episcopal Church, I preside over the Communion table. I have been set apart for that task by the laying on of hands by a bishop. I have been set apart further by the laying on of hands by the leadership of my congregation for a ministry of teaching within and out from that parish. But in recognition of the fact that my entire congregation is called to minister, most of them have received, through the laying on of hands by others, the anointing of the Holy Spirit to release their own gifts. The bishop lays hands on them at confirmation, and they are then ordained into their royal priesthood, in full view of the congregation. They may also have hands laid on them by others in prayer to discern a call to a specific ministry function or to release the power of the Spirit in their lives.

Each person has been given gifts for service by the Holy Spirit, without which our church would be impoverished. Have you ever heard of an anointing for cooking? We have had a succession of anointed men and women in the kitchen ministry. An anointing for child care? For printing the weekly bulletin? I don't believe that a church can realize its intended purpose until all of its members have discovered their gifts and received the anointing of the Holy Spirit to do what God has called them to do—until they are exercising, to some extent, the holy priesthood to which they have been commissioned by the laying on of hands.

The author of the book of Hebrews told his Jewish Christian readers that they were still spiritual babies. Then he listed the elementary doctrines they should already have mastered—repentance, faith, baptism, resurrection, eternal judgment, and the laying on of hands. Why did the early Church consider this so important? Because it was through the laying on of hands that they could recognize the God-given ministry of the people, and the Church could function as it was intended.

The laying on of hands in ministry also has precedence in the laying on of hands in blessing, which is first mentioned in terms of inheritance. "Israel reached out his right hand and put it on Ephraim's head," conferring a blessing and prophetic word (Genesis 48:14). Is not the setting apart for ministry within the Body of Christ one's spiritual inheritance? Will it not bring blessing to the Body as well as to the individual?

Jesus conferred His blessing upon children by placing His hands on them (see Matthew 19:15; Mark 10:16). We do this today when a child who is too young to receive the sacraments comes to the altar rail in the arms of a parent. The laying on of hands—it is a word of blessing, a means of receiving your spiritual inheritance and being set apart for ministry; it is a means by which you are made increasingly fit for God's presence.

Healing Hands

We also exercise our royal priesthood by laying hands on someone and praying for his or her healing. We do this because Jesus did. Mark 6:5 states that in Nazareth Jesus had a problem: "He could not do any miracles there, except lay his hands on a few sick people and heal them." Luke records: "When the sun was setting, the people brought to Jesus all who had various kinds of sickness, and laying his hands on each one, he healed them" (Luke 4:40).

After His resurrection, Jesus appeared to the apostles and sent them out into the world to preach the Good News. Jesus told them: "And these signs will accompany those who believe: In my name . . . they will place their hands on sick people, and they will get well" (Mark 16:17–18).

In the name of Jesus we pray for the sick and they are healed. Please understand two things about this: It is Jesus who heals, no matter whose hands are used, and He does not heal all the same way. Placing one's hands on another and praying for that person's healing is not a guaranteed technique that works unconditionally all the time. The person who places hands on another and prays for healing is doing two things: submitting himself or herself as a vessel to be used by God as He chooses, and bringing the person prayed for before the Lord to receive His blessing. God sovereignly chooses the blessing that person is to receive.

When we approach God, we do so knowing that He is omniscient, all-knowing, that we come before Him as imperfect vessels by the grace of Jesus Christ, and that we have no demands we can make from Him. We seek to be a part of whatever God has in mind for the particular person we pray for. Is there service that God wants that person to perform? He will provide the means to do so. Does He want the person to draw closer to Him? He will enable that process. There are as many variables in healing as there are people with spiritual, emotional, and physical needs for it. We must allow God to be God in the process.

This is where our sin nature—our unclean hands and impure hearts—gets in the way of our fitness to serve in God's presence. We must learn to pray with no agendas, no conditions, no expectations save that we and the person with whom we pray will be drawn closer to God and strengthened for whatever God has in store.

The Work of Our Hands

The Bible also speaks of being fit for God's presence by the "work of our hands." We might not think of our work as a means of growing spiritually—except perhaps as a test of our endurance! I want to help to change that concept.

Work was ordained by God back in Genesis 1. God did not put Adam and Eve in the Garden of Eden to enjoy the flora and the fauna. He gave them two tasks: to multiply and fill the earth, and to subdue the earth and have dominion over it.

After their disobedience (recorded in Genesis 3) Adam and Eve still had the same instructions, but with a difference. God told them that their work would now be difficult, accomplished by the sweat of the brow and pain. Had mankind not sinned, work would have been a wholly spiritual experience! (It is still possible, through Christ, to see it that way.) In any case, work is still part of the mandate given at creation, and a person's failure to work does not glorify God.

The apostle Paul, who supported himself in Thessalonica by tent making, later shared with the Thessalonians his observation that many in that congregation were not working but living in idleness. Maybe they were so spiritual that they wanted only to pray all the time? He wrote, "Such people we command and urge in the Lord

Jesus Christ to settle down and earn the bread they eat" (2 Thessalonians 3:12). Earlier he had given this important admonition: "Make it your ambition to lead a quiet life, to mind your own business and to work with your hands, just as we told you, so that your daily life may win the respect of outsiders and so that you will not be dependent on anybody" (1 Thessalonians 4:11–12).

The church is not a haven for idleness. Work is the command of the Lord, part of His plan for His people. Each of us is to work according to the abilities and gifts God has given us. The Bible stipulates three attitudes we should have toward our work: working for God's glory, working as if we were doing it for the Lord, and realizing that our success comes from God.

Paul wrote to the Corinthians: "So whether you eat or drink or whatever you do, do it all for the glory of God" (1 Corinthians 10:31). Can you do your job to the glory of God? If not, change jobs; it's as simple as that. If there's something out of line with God's glory about what you do, you're doing the wrong work. Peter expounded on this: "If anyone speaks, he should do it as one speaking the very words of God. If anyone serves, he should do it with the strength God provides, so that in all things God may be praised through Jesus Christ. To him be the glory and the power for ever and ever. Amen" (1 Peter 4:11).

We don't work for our earthly bosses. No matter what we do, whether we are the President of the United States or the bag boy at the grocery store, if we belong to Christ, we work for Jesus. He has set us apart to do whatever we do in His name. In the following passage, replace the words *slaves* and *masters* with *employees* and *employers:* "Slaves, obey your earthly masters with respect and fear, and with sincerity of heart, just as you would obey Christ. Obey them not only to win their favor when their eye is on you, but like slaves of Christ, doing the will of God from your heart" (Ephesians 6:5–6). Your work is to be done in reverence for Christ. Enter your workplace committed to doing what will honor Him.

It has always puzzled me when I hear people describe themselves in terms of their jobs. It goes something like this: "Hi, I'm Spike and I'm vice-president in charge of widgets at Such and Such, Incorporated." All of a sudden, you can see the computers in people's minds retrieving all the data as to what a V.P. in charge of widgets would be like. That then becomes the basis on which they relate to Spike at least initially.

Scripture warns us about taking our jobs as our identities. "You may say to yourself, 'My power and the strength of my hands have produced this wealth for me.' But remember the Lord your God, for it is he who gives you the ability to produce wealth, and so confirms his covenant, which he swore to your forefathers, as it is today" (Deuteronomy 8:17–18).

God has given us the ability to do whatever we accomplish. Perhaps it all comes down to realizing that the work of our hands is part of the work of God in the world. Paul wrote, "For we are God's fellow workers; you are God's field, God's building" (1 Corinthians 3:9). We work for God, with God, through God, to His glory.

Lift Up Your Hands

The Bible also speaks of our hands being lifted in worship to God. This ancient form of prayer is applicable in joy or sorrow. On one occasion, David exclaimed, "Because your love is better than life, my lips will glorify you. I will praise you as long as I live, and in your name I will lift up my hands" (Psalm 63:3–4). On another, he wrote, "Hear my cry for mercy as I call to you for help, as I lift up my hands toward your Most Holy Place" (Psalm 28:2). Jeremiah wrote in his anguish, "Arise, cry out in the night, as the watches of the night begin; pour out your heart like water in the presence of the Lord. Lift up your hands to him for the lives of your children, who faint from hunger at the head of every street" (Lamentations 2:19).

Scripture sounds a call for all God's people who stand in His house to lift up their hands to Him: "Praise the Lord, all you servants of the Lord who minister by night in the house of the Lord. Lift up your hands in the sanctuary and praise the Lord" (Psalm 134:1–2). Paul writes to Timothy of his desire: "I want men everywhere to lift up holy hands in prayer, without anger or disputing" (1 Timothy 2:8).

At the end of most church services, the minister pronounces some kind of blessing, symbolized by the raising of his hands. These days many are learning to stand in prayer with their hands, faces, and hearts raised to the Lord. It is the universal position of surrender—and a most appropriate exercise for spiritual fitness.

Summary

Let's thank God for the gift of our hands! They are cleansed and made fit for God's presence through the sacrifice of Jesus. They are to be used for His glory by making an offering, consecrating people for His service, bestowing His blessing, being a channel for His healing grace. They are to be used in our daily work to glorify Him, and to be lifted to Him in praise and worship.

Warm-Up Exercises

1. What soils your hands and makes you unfit for God's presence?

2. For what purpose have you had hands laid on you or laid hands on another?

3. God has set you apart to serve Him in your work. How does your attitude toward your work reflect this?

4. Why would people feel awkward lifting hands in prayer in public?

Stretching

Memorize Psalm 63:3–4 and practice lifting your hands to God daily: "Because your love is better than life, my lips will glorify you. I will praise you as long as I live, and in your name I will lift up my hands."

7

The Feet

Our feet are probably the most neglected parts of our bodies. Yet, as anyone who has had such trouble knows, if your foot hurts, you hurt all over—so important are feet to our physical sense of fitness.

Every day we subject our feet to tremendous pressure. They bear the weight of our bodies and the impact of our movements, and they are uniquely constructed by God for just that purpose.

The human foot has twenty-six bones that form three arches, two running lengthwise and one running across the instep. The arches provide the natural elastic spring of the foot as we walk or jump. A thick layer of flexible cartilage covers the ends of the bones of the arches, making them shock-absorbent. The arches are supported by ligaments and muscles, which protect the nerves and blood vessels in the hollow of the foot. The foot has as many muscles as the hand, but its structure permits less freedom of movement than the hand. A tough, thick skin covers the bottom of the foot, which is a thick pad of fatty tissue. This layer of fat acts like an air cushion to protect the inner parts of the foot from pressure and from jarring.

In terms of our spiritual fitness, the importance of our feet is seen in their ability to carry us on the path of righteousness—or on the path of rebellion. Proverbs puts it this way: "Make level paths for your feet and take only ways that are firm. Do not swerve to the right or the left; keep your foot from evil" (Proverbs 4:26–27).

The New Testament parallels this admonition: "Look carefully then how you walk, not as unwise men but as wise, making the most of the time, because the days are evil" (Ephesians 5:15–16, RSV).

Because some of the decisions we make have consequences that reach further than is immediately discernible, the Bible cautions us to pay close attention to the direction we go and the path we take. In this regard, God has given us three promises and seven exhortations having to do with our feet, spiritually speaking.

Promises

Let's first look at the promises God makes to His people.

God Promises Deliverance

I waited patiently for the Lord; he turned to me and heard my cry. He lifted me out of the slimy pit, out of the mud and mire; he set my feet on a rock and gave me a firm place to stand.   Psalm 40:1–2

When we have slipped into the mire of sin and can't get ourselves out, God promises to deliver us if we wait patiently for Him. Please understand, the waiting that God expects from us is not passive, as if we were waiting for a bus. *Waiting for the Lord* refers to the active sense of waiting *on* Him, as His servant. This involves honoring His name, seeking Him continually, following His instructions. That's how we will be lifted from the pit of desolation and placed on solid rock. To have our feet "set upon a rock" means that He will place us upon the Rock, the Lord Jesus Christ, where our footing is sure. Paul writes of the experience of Israel: "They all ate the same spiritual food and drank the same spiritual drink; for they drank from the spiritual rock that accompanied them, and that rock was Christ" (1 Corinthians 10:3–4). Throughout Scripture, God's work in the lives of His people commenced as an act of deliverance. For example, God delivered the children of Israel out of bondage in Egypt, into the land of promise. So it is with us: God promises to lift us from bondage to selfishness, sin, and death into freedom, life, and peace.

God Promises Strength

> Do you not know? Have you not heard? The Lord is the everlasting God, the Creator of the ends of the earth. He will not grow tired or weary, and his understanding no one can fathom. . . . But those who hope in the Lord will renew their strength. They will soar on wings like eagles; they will run and not grow weary, they will walk and not be faint.   Isaiah 40:28, 31

Here God is not promising that those who follow Him will never be tired, as He never tires. Rather, He is promising that their strength will be constantly renewed—like a rechargeable razor. Though my own razor carries within it enough power to last nearly a month, it eventually runs down and needs to be recharged. God promises us a similar recharging whenever we "plug in" to His strength, so that we can, as He said, soar like eagles.

Eagles don't fly, except when they are taking off from level ground. They fasten their feet to the edge of a cliff and stand poised for flight until the right wind comes along. When it does, they let go and soar with the air currents, rising higher and higher, banking to the right or left. Because they have an inborn understanding of air currents, eagles are borne aloft by the wind.

The Hebrew and Greek words for *spirit—ruach* and *pneuma—*are also translated *wind*, providing a graphic physical parallel to the spiritual life. Just as eagles are borne along by the wind, so Christians can catch the direction of God's Spirit, let go, and soar.

What a difference between living in the power of the flesh, with all its wing-flapping commotion, and living in the power of the Spirit—being borne aloft by God's power! Any believer who thinks that his or her own energy can yield effective spiritual results should hear the words of the prophet Zechariah: " 'Not by might nor by power, but by my Spirit,' says the Lord Almighty" (4:6b).

God Promises Guidance

> I know, O Lord, that a man's life is not his own; it is not for man to direct his steps.   Jeremiah 10:23

This has both a negative and positive aspect. On the negative side, we must recognize that we will never grow to the point of self-sufficiency, no matter how mature we become in our faith. Far from it! The more we learn of God's ways, the more we realize that we do not possess the requisite wisdom to choose the right paths for our feet to follow. No wonder so many people are confused; unaware that God wants to direct their steps, they are functioning under the limitations of their own understanding. That's true of Christians, too.

Many churches and parachurch organizations believe that the effectiveness of their ministries depends upon the resourcefulness of the people on their governing boards. They assemble the best minds available, thinking those wise in the world will be able to direct their work properly. They count on intelligence and experience, never realizing that the banker in their midst may know lots about money but very little about the ways of the Lord. I do not demean skill and expertise and their value to the Body of Christ. I only emphasize that our ways are not God's ways; we can never in the flesh direct our paths according to the wisdom of God.

If we have not yet committed our lives to Jesus and the Holy Spirit does not reside in us, we are limited to our own resources. The Holy Spirit, the Wisdom of God, knows God's will infallibly and will guide all who turn to Him. That brings us to the positive side of the promise of God's guidance: "Trust in the Lord with all your heart and lean not on your own understanding; in all your ways acknowledge him, and he will make your paths straight" (Proverbs 3:5–6).

Scripture promises guidance to those who are ready to trust in God, to rely on Him, not their own limited understanding. To some people, that sounds like bad advice. "What do you mean, I'm not to trust in my own understanding? I've got a Ph.D. from Harvard!" God does not mean that we are not to use the intelligence He has given us and to sharpen it through constant use and education. We're just not to consider our intelligence infallible. We must not rely on ourselves but on God. Then, as we make His will our goal, He promises to make our paths straight.

Exhortations

Having received three promises from God, we need to know of seven exhortations related to our feet making us fit for God's presence.

Walk in Newness of Life

> Don't you know that all of us who were baptized into Christ Jesus were baptized into his death? We were therefore buried with him through baptism into death in order that, just as Christ was raised from the dead through the glory of the Father, we too may live a new life.
>
> Romans 6:3–4

Some churches baptize by sprinkling, some by pouring, some by total immersion. In this Romans passage, the image points to immersion, in which the candidate is dipped completely under the water. In that sense, the person is considered to have "died"—been buried under the waves of water and resurrected alive up from it. That image illustrates an important truth in our Christian experience. If we have opened our hearts to Jesus, in a real sense we have already died. We have died to ourselves. Paul goes on to write: "In the same way, count yourselves dead to sin but alive to God in Christ Jesus" (verse 11). If we identify with Christ in His death, everything in us that is not in harmony with God's will has died. Consequently, we are identified with Christ and His resurrection, and we are able to live a new life.

Walk in Good Works

> For we are God's workmanship, created in Christ Jesus to do good works, which God prepared in advance for us to do.   Ephesians 2:10

The Christian life is a process in which God is at work in us. The good works that God has prepared for us to do are done only by God working in us to produce the kind of fruit that He desires. The fact that God has a plan for our lives, however, is not a guarantee that we will ever fulfill it. God has given us free will, and, if we choose, we can live our entire lives apart from His plan. Tragically, multitudes of people live and die without knowing God even *has* such a plan. It is even more tragic to think that many who have attended church all their lives have not been told that God has a whole series of good works prepared for them. It is not a new concept! This is a truth that David acknowledged some three thousand years ago: "All the days ordained for me were written in your book before one of them came to be" (Psalm 139:16b).

What a graphic picture of the diary God has for each of our lives! A page for each day, on which He has recorded the good works He has planned for us. I wonder: On how many of them has He had to write, "unfulfilled because of willfulness"? His plan for us involves a whole life of good works that He will open up for us if we are yielded to Him, and that we will miss if we refuse Him.

Walk in the Light

> But if we walk in the light, as he is in the light, we have fellowship with one another, and the blood of Jesus, his Son, purifies us from all sin.
> If we claim to be without sin, we deceive ourselves and the truth is not in us. If we confess our sins, he is faithful and just and will forgive us our sins and purify us from all unrighteousness. If we claim we have not sinned, we make him out to be a liar and his word has no place in our lives.
>   1 John 1:7–10

This exhortation is based on the transparent character of God. There are no shadows in His being. He is light through and through. If we walk with Him, our lives are transformed by His light.

Our natural tendency, ever since Adam and Eve, is to cover up our sins. We want to choose our own paths, to live according to our own desires, to hide from the face of God. But if we want to walk with God, who is Light, we must walk in His light, which means we can't gloss over our sins. We must face the things in our lives that are out of harmony with God's purpose. We must stop rationalizing wrong attitudes and justifying wrongdoing, and we must call sin what God calls sin. To do this accurately, we must line up our lives with His Word. David writes, "Your word is a lamp to my feet and a light for my path" (Psalm 119:105).

If God's Word says we have sinned, we need to confess that sin. Sin is not an insurmountable problem for God. Even the most abhorrent sin we can imagine has been dealt with by the atoning death of the Lord Jesus Christ.

We are prevented from receiving God's forgiveness only when we refuse to confess our sins. There is a false idea making the rounds of ecclesiastical circles today suggesting that God automatically forgives sin, without repentance. This is not true. We receive the forgiveness of God when we are willing to agree with God—that what He calls sin is our sin—and repent of it.

I have met people who are worried that they haven't made a clean confession. They fear that there is something they may have forgotten and for which God will hold them eternally accountable. I tell them that, if they walk in the light of Christ, their sins will be obvious to them and they will be able to deal with them. If a sin hasn't surfaced yet, don't go fishing. Don't look for sins that you *might* have committed. Rather, deal with the ones God brings to your attention.

Walking in the light requires that we keep short accounts with God. Don't wait until Sunday if you are convicted by the Holy Spirit on Wednesday. As soon as you become aware of a wrong action or attitude, deal with it immediately—confess it and receive God's forgiveness. As a result, we will receive both His forgiveness and the fellowship with one another that He promises.

The father of John the Baptizer, describing the promise of Jesus said: "Because of the tender mercy of our God . . . the rising sun will come to us from heaven to shine on those living in darkness and in the shadow of death, to guide our feet into the path of peace" (Luke 1:78–79).

Walk in Love

> This is how we know that we love the children of God: by loving God and carrying out his commands. This is love for God: to obey his commands. And his commands are not burdensome, for everyone born of God overcomes the world. This is the victory that has overcome the world, even our faith.   1 John 5:2–4

The word *love* is abused by our culture. We can love God and pizza at the same time. The Bible gives a precise meaning to the word *love*—both for God and for one another. Simply put, *love* is "keeping the commandments of God." If we love God, we demonstrate it by our obedience to Him. We cannot love God and violate His will. This doesn't mean we will be perfect beings. It means that if we love God, our greatest concern in life is to discover His will and purpose for us; when we fail to live up to His standards, we confess it, receive His forgiveness, and start over.

If we love one another, we are to act lovingly toward one another. We can't generate a feeling of warmth toward people we don't especially like, but we can act in a loving way, whether or not we like them and regardless of how they act.

Walk in Liberty

> I will always obey your law, for ever and ever. I will walk about in freedom, for I have sought out your precepts.
> Psalm 119:44–45

Walking in liberty is a paradox. Our freedom, which has limits, is found in obedience. Many people think liberty is the absence of constraint, the ability to do whatever they want, when they want to do it, without any form of accountability. Nothing could be further from the truth. In fact, living according to that philosophy brings us into incredible bondage.

Liberty, as described in the pages of the New Testament, is living in harmony with God. It gives us a sense of joy, of purposefulness, of the fulfilling of God's plan for us. Walking in new life, walking in good works, walking in the light, walking in love—all of these are possible only if we are walking in obedience. That's walking in liberty.

I recall a children's story about a train that was unhappy

because it had to stay on the track rather than wander around the countryside. One day the train derailed and couldn't go anywhere. Only then did it understand that the track, which had seemed so restrictive, had actually been the very means by which it could move smoothly from place to place.

The commandments of God are the tracks on which we are able to move. We might consider them oppressive and binding, but when we live our lives in harmony with God's commandments, we discover an exhilarating sense of freedom, like that found by the "rerailed" train. We were created to function joyfully under the law of God, and, when we do so, we discover the liberty He has promised.

Walk in Humility

He has showed you, O man, what is good. And what does the Lord require of you? To act justly and to love mercy and to walk humbly with your God.   Micah 6:8

Walking humbly with God is not an exercise in poor self-esteem. It is rather the knowledge that God resists human pride.

Imagine how uncomfortable the disciples must have felt during the Last Supper when Jesus removed His garment, took a towel, and assumed the menial role of a slave washing their feet. Each of them had taken pains to avoid performing this duty for the others. Jesus was saying that no service is ever too low to be considered appropriate for one of His disciples. Walking humbly with our God means that no practical ministry is ever beneath us. When we are secure in our identities as children of God, no service is too humble for us to perform for another in the name of the Lord.

Walk in the Spirit

Since we live by the Spirit, let us keep in step with the Spirit.   Galatians 5:25

It is the Holy Spirit who gives God's life to us and takes up residence within us. Maintaining a life that is pleasing to God, becoming fit for His presence, we must fulfill His admonition to walk in step with the power of the Spirit. Unless we do, fulfilling the other six admonitions will be impossible.

Summary

Feet fit for God's presence. I pray that, by claiming His promises and following His admonitions, each of us will be able to say with the psalmist: "For you have delivered my soul from death and my feet from stumbling, that I may walk before God in the light of life" (Psalm 56:13).

Warm-Up Exercises

1. Which of God's promises would you like to see realized in your life?

2. Which of the seven exhortations do you feel you have difficulty following?

3. How closely do you feel you are following the path God has prepared for you?

4. What steps do you need to take to walk in the Spirit?

Stretching

Memorize Psalm 56:13 as a promise for your life: "For you have delivered my soul from death and my feet from stumbling, that I may walk before God in the light of life."

8

The Heart

The media today loves to talk about the fitness of the heart. They warn us about cholesterol levels, salt intake, and smoking. They encourage us to walk, jog, or engage in other aerobic exercise. They give us tips on how to reduce stress. We are becoming an increasingly "heart-conscious" society.

What is the reason for all of this? Our heart is the center of our physical being. Without its function, we cease to exist. All people, regardless of the other contributing factors, ultimately die from cardiac arrest—the cessation of the beating of the heart.

The heartbeat we hear is actually the sound of the organ pumping out blood, which carries oxygen that the brain and other parts of the body need to live. If your heart stops, the oxygen is cut off and you will die unless a special device is used to circulate your blood. That's a very important function for a hollow muscle that is no bigger than your fist! Your fist and your heart grow at the same rate.

The Bible is concerned with the fitness of our hearts, too. The heart spoken of in Scripture is not the heart that pumps blood, but rather everything that makes us what we are. It includes our intellect, imagination, will, intentions, thoughts, memory, emotions. When Scripture says we are to love God with all our heart, soul, mind, and strength, it refers to the totality of the human personality.

Think of the terminology Scripture uses to indicate heart attitudes: *Broken-hearted, faint-hearted, hard-hearted, heartless* —all leave us with a heartache. *Kind-hearted, simple-hearted, stout-hearted,* and *wholehearted* imply that a change of heart has occurred. If the heart is corrupted, the whole person is corrupted. If the heart is glad, the whole person is glad.

Let's look at our spiritual heart fitness in three ways: Its transparency before God, its damage by universal heart disease, and its healthy attitudes before the Lord.

Transparent Hearts

We have learned that God sees beyond the outward appearance of things. His eyes peer directly into the center of our beings; He knows our hearts. As He told the prophet Samuel: "The Lord does not look at the things man looks at. Man looks at the outward appearance, but the Lord looks at the heart" (1 Samuel 16:7b).

King David understood this and gave his son and heir a wonderful piece of advice: "And you, my son Solomon, acknowledge the God of your father, and serve him with wholehearted devotion and with a willing mind, for the Lord searches every heart and understands every motive behind the thoughts" (1 Chronicles 28:9a).

Nothing passes through our minds that is not perfectly open to the Lord God. As far as He is concerned, our innermost thoughts might as well be broadcast on the national news! The writer of the book of Hebrews warns: "Nothing in all creation is hidden from God's sight. Everything is uncovered and laid bare before the eyes of him to whom we must give account" (Hebrews 4:13).

Some find this idea frightening—that God's vision pierces the deepest recesses of our hearts to things that we have kept concealed, even from ourselves. It should be frightening to those who are hiding from God, but comforting to those who wish to serve Him.

I once saw a Christian TV show on which a nun was telling of her strict upbringing and parochial education. Her parents and teachers had used the concept of an omniscient God to frighten her into good behavior; she had grown up terrified of the all-seeing eye of God. Then the person with whom she was speaking exclaimed, "My dear sister, you've got it all wrong! God does see you all the time, but it's because He loves you so much He can't take His eyes off you!" What a beautiful perspective of God's penetrating vision!

Trying to hide from Him is an exercise in futility. Is there anywhere we can hide from the Almighty who created the universe? The psalmist says no. "Where can I go from your Spirit? Where can I flee from your presence? If I go up to the heavens, you are there; if I make my bed in the depths, you are there. If I rise on the wings of the dawn, if I settle on the far side of the sea, even there your hand will guide me, your right hand will hold me fast" (Psalm 139:7–10).

Can we really hope to avoid Him by engaging in ceaseless rounds of activity? Can we expect to lose Him in the crowd of humanity? Fleeing from God (in an endless variety of ways) is the universal reaction of human beings aware of their sin. It began with Adam and Eve; what the serpent called "wisdom" made them aware of their nakedness, and they were ashamed and hid from God. Throughout the ages it has remained the same. Genesis 6 describes the human race generations after Adam and Eve, before God's judgment by the flood in the time of Noah: "The Lord saw how great man's wickedness on the earth had become, and that every inclination of the thoughts of his heart was only evil all the time. The Lord was grieved that he had made man on the earth, and his heart was filled with pain" (verses 5–6). God's heart is still filled with pain over human hearts that are "only evil all the time."

Universal Heart Disease

Starting with the book of Genesis, the Bible does not present a flattering view of human nature. In some ways, Scripture seems to take great pains to paint a negative picture. Many protest, "But I'm a nice person!" when being confronted with Paul's statement (quoting from the Psalms) that says, "There is no one righteous, not even one" (Romans 3:10b). But the Bible describes how we really are on the inside, not how we wish we were. All of us have diseased spiritual hearts.

There are several symptoms of this universal heart disease. Struggle, deceit, wrongful motivation, and hypocrisy are all forms of spiritual plaque that clog our spiritual arteries. I want us to look at each one, so we can recognize each symptom and get help before it gets out of hand.

Struggle

There is a universal war that goes on within every heart between what we know we ought to do and what we actually do. The apostle Paul wrote: "I do not understand what I do. For what I want to do I do not do, but what I hate I do. . . . For I have the desire to do what is good, but I cannot carry it out. For what I do is not the good I want to do; no, the evil I do not want to do—this I keep on doing" (Romans 7:15, 18b–19).

The acknowledgment of this struggle is not limited to Judeo-Christian thinking. Marcus Aurelius, the Stoic philosopher-emperor, wrote in a moving passage that, despite educational and other advantages, he discovered something wrong inside himself that he did not understand. Eastern philosophers, while using a different language, also recognize something fundamentally wrong with humanity. All of the religions of the world have developed as ways to deal with that universal symptom.

Theologians put their own name to it: original sin. They agree with Scripture that every part of the inner being, as well as the physical body, is affected by the inclination toward wrongdoing. The problems of society, the problems of the world, are only results of this universal heart disease. Our Lord's brother wrote: "What causes fights and quarrels among you? Don't they come from your desires that battle within you? You want something but don't get it. You kill and covet, but you cannot have what you want. You quarrel and fight. You do not have, because you do not ask God" (James 4:1–2).

Deceit

We don't like to face this truth, so we build up defense mechanisms and rationales to justify our behavior. This is the second symptom. Jeremiah calls it what it is—deceit. "The heart is deceitful above all things and beyond cure. Who can understand it?" (Jeremiah 17:9). Then comes the answer: "I the Lord search the heart and examine the mind, to reward a man according to his conduct, according to what his deeds deserve" (verse 10).

It is natural to try to prove someone else wrong so we can be right, to make ourselves look as good as possible. We don't have to teach our children these things; they learn them instinctively. Again, it started with Adam and Eve. When God said to Adam, "Who told you that you were naked? Have you eaten from the tree that I commanded you not to eat from?" Adam's reply was, "The woman you put here with me—she gave me some fruit from the tree, and I ate it" (Genesis 3:11–12). Adam was rationalizing: "It's not my fault, God. It's Eve's. She gave me the apple." Or, "Really, God, it's Your fault. You put her here. I didn't ask You to do that."

But God sees through the rationalizing to the inner workings of our hearts. He observes it all. He sees the motives behind the words. He hears the distortions and sees the perspectives we create.

Only as we are able to accept that picture of ourselves, as broken and separated from a holy God, will we understand our need for forgiveness. Why did God have to go to such lengths to save us? Why did He have to send Jesus into the world to die in our place? Because He recognized our true condition as deceivers, even of ourselves.

Wrongful Motivation

Another symptom of universal heart disease is wrongful motivation. Different branches of psychiatric theory would agree that much of our motivation (or desire) originates below the conscious level. Though we may be aware of a surfacing desire, we are not necessarily aware of its origin or reason. But Jesus pinpointed the origen: "For out of the heart come evil thoughts, murder, adultery, sexual immorality, theft, false testimony, slander" (Matthew 15:19).

The Lord's brother, in an acute psychological analysis of temptation, taught that wrong desire starts in the heart long before it mushrooms into actions.

> When tempted, no one should say, "God is tempting me." For God cannot be tempted by evil, nor does he tempt anyone; but each one is tempted when, by his own evil desire, he is dragged away and enticed. Then, after desire has conceived, it gives birth to sin; and sin, when it is full-grown, gives birth to death.   James 1:13–15

The desire to sin is not the same thing as a sinful action. Jesus Himself was "tempted in every way, just as we are—yet was without sin" (Hebrews 4:15b). Temptation becomes sin only when we dwell on the desire until it conceives and gives birth to a sinful act. God does not tempt us in order to test us. Temptation comes from our own motivation.

Jesus asked us to consider our inward motivations before they have a chance to become sinful acts. The sins He named—evil thoughts, murder, adultery, sexual immorality, theft, lying, slander—are all manifestations of feelings, thoughts, and intentions that arise in the heart.

You may never have murdered anyone, but, if you understand Jesus correctly in the Sermon on the Mount, He judged hatred as harshly as murder. Why? Because the act of murder is conceived as hatred long before it becomes an act. Many more murders would be committed if people were not afraid of the consequences. This confirms the Bible's diagnosis of universal heart disease.

Hypocrisy

Hypocrisy is the fourth symptom of universal heart disease. Hypocrisy is the outward appearance of something that is far different from the inward reality. Jesus leveled the following charge of hypocrisy against the religious leaders of His day:

> "Woe to you, teachers of the law and Pharisees, you hypocrites! You are like whitewashed tombs, which look beautiful on the outside but on the inside are full of dead men's bones and everything unclean. In the same way, on the outside you appear to people as righteous but on the inside you are full of hypocrisy and wickedness."
>
> Matthew 23:27–28

Humanity is the only part of God's creation that has the capacity to act one way while feeling the opposite. A cat reacts like a cat, a dog like a dog; they are predictable to a certain extent. But, because God gave us free will, the freedom to choose our actions and reactions, we are not predictable. Hypocrisy is a choice that we make—to try to look better than we know we are.

Heart Transplant for a Healthy Heart

Is it not obvious that we all have the symptoms of advanced spiritual heart disease and are in desperate need of heart transplants? Our sinful nature in its various manifestations has caused a spiritual arteriosclerosis—a hardening and narrowing that restricts the flow of God's life in and through us. We need spiritual transplants in which our stony, unrepentant, self-justifying hearts are taken out and replaced with pliable, soft, living hearts that respond to God. God is the only One who can do this delicate surgery, and He promises to do it instantly, painlessly, and free of charge! "I will give you a new heart and put a new spirit in you; I will remove from you your heart of stone and give you a heart of flesh. And I will put my Spirit in you and move you to follow my decrees and be careful to keep my laws" (Ezekiel 36:26–27).

Believe

How? Well, the preparation for surgery is threefold. The first step is to believe. "If you confess with your mouth, 'Jesus is Lord,' and believe in your heart that God raised him from the dead, you will be saved. For it is with your heart that you believe and are justified, and it is with your mouth that you confess and are saved" (Romans 10:9–10). This is more than giving a mental assent to Jesus' Lordship. Even demons know He is Lord. One could sign some theological statement agreeing intellectually with Jesus' Lordship as revealed in Scripture and never once experience the reality of a personal relationship with Him. Many in the Church today do just that! We are being asked here to believe with our whole beings—first with our minds, then with our emotions, feelings, and wills. Once we have done that, it is easy to move on to the next preoperative step—confession.

Confess Our Sins

We need to confess our sinful nature. This may be a difficult thing to do; we may feel as if our spiritual hearts are broken in the process. Scripture commends that: "The sacrifices of God are a broken spirit; a broken and contrite heart, O God, you will not despise" (Psalm 51:17). When we accept the truth of God's description of our spiritual condition and don't try to hide it, we can confess and offer our broken, wounded, contrite hearts to God. Try it! Not just once, but many times over. It's both a presurgical condition and postoperative maintenance. Whenever you feel you have wandered from God, offer that realization to Him. Give Him your sense of failure, your shame, and know that the acknowledgment of your condition is a sacrifice acceptable in His sight.

Confess Jesus' Lordship

After you've confessed your sins, you need to confess your need of Jesus Christ as Savior. One should do this publicly if at all possible, as the Romans 10 passage suggests. But if you are not ready to make a public declaration, don't delay confessing Him as Lord! Salvation is just as wonderful if it is done in the quietness of your heart. At some point when you are ready to make a public confession, the opportunity will arise for you to do so. Publicly or quietly, whenever you accept Jesus Christ as personal Savior, asking Him to "come into your heart," He does just that and your spiritual heart transplant is completed.

That's just the beginning of the daily regimen necessary to keep the new heart healthy and to keep the old spiritual heart disease from infecting the new heart. How do we keep our hearts free from spiritual plaque build up?

Heart Maintenance

One way is to keep our hearts seeking God. We need to study the Word of God daily, seeking Him and His will for us as a daily dose of anti-rejection medication. "The word of God is living and active. Sharper than any double-edged sword, it penetrates even to dividing soul and spirit, joints and marrow; it judges the thoughts and attitudes of the heart" (Hebrews 4:12).

This medication does have a side effect, however. When we choose to seek God, our hearts are filled with great joy. "Glory in his holy name; let the hearts of those who seek the Lord rejoice" (1 Chronicles 16:10).

And, of course, after surgery we need to have periodic checkups: "Search me, O God, and know my heart; test me and know my anxious thoughts. See if there is any offensive way in me, and lead me in the way everlasting" (Psalm 139:23–24). We need to be willing to open our hearts to God's inspection. This involves an attitude that invites Him to bring to our attention those things that are offensive to Him—things we may not even remember, the memory of which may be a bit uncomfortable. But, over time, we will find that our new hearts give us a life of peace, joy, wholeness, and power that we never thought possible.

Summary

I want to conclude with a wonderful promise: "For the eyes of the Lord range throughout the earth to strengthen those whose hearts are fully committed to him" (2 Chronicles 16:9a).

Now, none of us has a heart fully committed to Him. But what God seeks is a heart committed to being committed to Him, one broken and contrite, whose attitudes invite the searching gaze of the Holy Spirit. Is it in you? If so, God wants to strengthen you. He longs to make you fit for His presence, so He can bless you and give you abundant life.

In times of frustration, I have found that we discover the good things God promises only as we position ourselves under the Lordship of Jesus Christ, our individual head and head of the Body of Christ. He is Lord—whether or not we acknowledge Him!

As we personally accept His Lordship, our spiritual hearts pump the peace that passes understanding; they beat to the rhythm of God's blessing in our lives; the joy of the Lord courses through our bodies and gives us a surge of supernatural power. That's a heart fit for God's presence.

Warm-Up Exercises

1. How did you feel when you first realized that nothing in your life was hidden from God?

2. What symptoms of universal heart disease are currently manifesting themselves in your life?

3. Have you allowed God to perform a spiritual heart transplant?

4. If so, how is the after-surgery regimen going?

Stretching

Memorize Psalm 139:23–24 and use it as a daily prayer to God: "Search me, O God, and know my heart; test me and know my anxious thoughts. See if there is any offensive way in me, and lead me in the way everlasting."

Avoiding Stress

We cannot live in this world and not encounter stress in some form. In fact, we need some stress to keep us growing.

It is our reaction to stress that is dangerous. The medical community has come to recognize that our reaction to stress is a factor in many of the diseases that afflict us; in some cases, our stress reactions are treated as a disease in themselves.

Stress is also a fact of the spiritual life. Actually, it is on the spiritual level that we can learn to cope with the stress in our lives, so that our physical fitness also benefits. For us to understand how this is done, we need to spend a little time with the apostle Paul.

Stress Levels

If there was one thing Paul knew about, it was a stressful Christian life. His conversion was, after all, quite dramatic: being thrown from his horse on the road to Damascus; meeting Jesus in a flash of bright light; being left blind and led by the hand to the city where he remained; fasting for three days, until a quaking Ananias came to pray for him to receive his sight. Paul should have had a clue at the beginning that his life was about to change from that of a secure citizen of both Rome and Israel.

History says that Paul was held in suspicion by the early Church—and why not? He had been a persecutor of

Christians. But when he was befriended by Barnabas, he embarked on missionary journeys that established churches. Read what he writes to one of the churches he founded about the stress level of his life in Christ:

> I have worked much harder, been in prison more frequently, been flogged more severely, and been exposed to death again and again. Five times I received from the Jews the forty lashes minus one. Three times I was beaten with rods, once I was stoned, three times I was shipwrecked, I spent a night and a day in the open sea, I have been constantly on the move. I have been in danger from rivers, in danger from bandits, in danger from my own countrymen, in danger from Gentiles; in danger in the city, in danger in the country, in danger at sea; and in danger from false brothers. I have labored and toiled and have often gone without sleep; I have known hunger and thirst and have often gone without food; I have been cold and naked. Besides everything else, I face daily the pressure of my concern for all the churches.
>
> 2 Corinthians 11:23b–28

Talk about stressful circumstances! It makes me wonder where those who developed the prosperity doctrine of modern Christianity ever found evidence for saying that if you believe in Christ, life will become rosy. Paul goes on to say, "Who is weak, and I do not feel weak? Who is led into sin, and I do not inwardly burn? If I must boast, I will boast of the things that show my weakness" (verses 29–30). He goes on to speak of a "thorn in the flesh" that he was dealing with.

> Three times I pleaded with the Lord to take it away from me. But he said to me, "My grace is sufficient for you, for my power is made perfect in weakness." Therefore I will boast all the more gladly about my weaknesses, so that Christ's power may rest on me. That is why, for Christ's sake, I delight in weaknesses, in insults, in hardships, in

persecutions, in difficulties. For when I am weak, then I
am strong.   2 Corinthians 12:8–10

Imagine someone saying, "I delight in weaknesses, in
hardships, in persecutions, in difficulties." Today we
would label that person a masochist and send him to the
nearest psychiatric treatment center. But Paul had experienced a deeper truth in his hardships—that God's grace
was sufficient, that God's power was made perfect in the
weakest points of his life. That realization is the first step
to spiritual stress management. Give God charge of it!

What causes a stress-filled reaction in you? There are
lists available that give stress ratings for some of the
common experiences of life. High on the list are the death
of a spouse or loved one, a move, a job change—the things
that totally change your life. The problems of life fall into
certain categories, and Scripture has something to say
about each of them. Come before the Lord in prayer and
ask Him to shine the light of His Spirit on your life, so that
you know what it is that is troubling you. Then get a Bible
concordance and read through all of the Scriptures listed
under that subject. The will of the Lord soon becomes
evident, and you can usually find where the point of stress
is for you. Give it to the Lord!

God has created you. He knows your limitations far
better than you do. Problems with stress are caused when
we exceed our God-given limitations. Inviting God to take
charge of the situations of our lives is saying, "Okay,
Lord. I trust You rather than myself on this." Release it to
Him. Take your hands off of it. Then, praise Him for
taking it—and take a deep calming breath.

Content Whatever Comes

Let's look at a part of another of Paul's letters, one
written to the Philippians. It was written from a familiar
stress-producing setting for Paul: jail. I've been to that jail,

opposite the Roman Forum, just behind the hill on which a great monument to Victor Emmanuel has been constructed. The jail is small, dark, and depressing. There would not have been room for more than the guard, Paul, and perhaps the person to whom he dictated his letter. Yet that hole was a chamber of glory; out of it came a letter full of love, joy, peace, and confidence—not one word of despair.

At the end of his letter, Paul thanks the Philippians for their concern for him, and in that thank-you note lies the key to his stress management:

> I am not saying this because I am in need, for I have *learned to be content whatever the circumstances.* I know what it is to be in need, and I know what it is to have plenty. I have learned the secret of being *content in any and every situation,* whether well fed or hungry, whether living in plenty or in want. I can do everything through him who gives me strength.   Philippians 4:11–13, italics added

Content in any and every situation. No one is exempt from problems in life. We sometimes say if we were millionaires our problems would be solved. Some would, but others would open up. Here Paul says, "I've learned how to cope with all of life. I've learned how to live in the low moments, when people don't appreciate or understand me, when they've turned against me, when things aren't going my way and all looks dark." Think of it!

People react to adversity in many ways. Some are filled with anger and strike back. Some are filled with resentment and bitterness, and it poisons their whole lives. But Paul says, "I've learned the secret of life. I've been to the cellar of life and I can be content there. I can also be content in a penthouse!"

Sometimes I think it's more difficult to live in plenty. There is something abut the cushion of success, that no matter how much we have, we never seem to have enough. I recall a question once asked of John D. Rock-efeller, Sr. He was asked, "How much money does it take to be satisfied?" His reply was, "More than I have." But Jesus said that a person's life does not consist of the abundance of possessions. If you measure your life by what you own, you will be constantly striving, constantly under stress.

The same applies to professional status. If you seek recognition and reward from the world for your talents and efforts, you will never receive enough acclaim. You'll never be satisfied with your job, with your salary, with the kind of house you live in. We cannot find contentment in the world. God has made us that way. Only He can provide that contentment that stays through any circumstance.

I'm not saying that this world does not provide its satisfactory moments. It does! But can we say, as Paul did, that we have learned how to live close to God in moments of prosperity? Can we say that our spiritual lives are strong when everything is going our way, when people speak well of us? Do we acknowledge Him as strongly when our talents are being amply rewarded? Do we thank Him when we can see the success of our labors? Do we give Him all the credit when we are being admired for our accomplishments?

Most don't. They give God credit for helping them out of trouble but take the credit when things are going well. Yet Paul says, "I've learned to handle my successes as well as my failures." When success comes, we begin to assume that life will always be lived at this level or higher, that there is nowhere to go but up. That's a trap that leads to discouragement and disappointment. But, Paul says, "I've learned how to handle it. I've learned to be content."

Learning to Be Content

The word translated *content* in that verse is significant because it appears nowhere else in the New Testament.

Paul, an educated man, chose to use a Greek technical word from the Stoic philosophy. Stoics took their name from the *stoa*, the porch or colonnade where they met. The stoics believed that happiness and contentment in life were things to be desired. They would have admired this statement of Paul, that he had learned to be content in whatever state he found himself. But there were light years of difference between contentment as Stoics understood it and the contentment of which Paul was speaking.

Stoics believed that each man had within himself reason, which related him to all others and to the universe. This belief provided a theoretical basis for cosmopolitanism, the idea that people are citizens of the world rather than a single nation or area. This view also stimulated the belief in a natural law that stood above civil law and provided a standard by which laws could be judged. The Stoics felt that man achieved his greatest good—happiness—by following reason, freeing himself from passions, and concentrating only on things he could control. They believed, in other words, that the way to contentment was to grit your teeth, clench your fist, and persevere. They decided they could get through anything by sheer determination.

There were two things in humanity that you had to overcome, according to the Stoics. First, you were to kill any desire at all. The Stoics observed that most people's unhappiness was caused by their desire for things that they did not get. That is a reasonable observation. Their solution to this was simply not to desire anything. If you desire nothing, you won't be disappointed.

The other Stoic belief was that you had to put to death every human emotion. Everything you love has the potential of injuring you, so the solution is not to love. Do you love a pet? Well, you'd be terribly hurt if the pet died, so don't love it. Family and friends? Don't love them, because they can hurt you. Kill any vestige of emotion in yourself and you will have contentment.

Contentment the Stoic way was purchased at a high cost. It stripped away human aspects that God had built into the personality of each one of us. Our ability to love and to desire are all attributes of God.

That kind of contentment was not what Paul was talking about. Paul loved. He loved deeply! He had great desires. All of this is readily evident in his letters. He did not lay aside those loves and desires to find contentment. He learned contentment by realizing that through the Lord Jesus Christ, he could have complete peace of mind. He could, through Jesus, detach himself from the circumstances around him so that whatever happened did not change his trust. He had complete confidence in Christ, and that brought about contentment.

Confidence and Coping

How did he learn that? Let's continue to look at the book of Philippians and consider some of the ways Paul expressed his confidence. "For to me, to live is Christ and to die is gain" (1:21). In other words, he said, "My life is Jesus Christ." Jesus was the foundation of his life, the goal of his life. Jesus was the substance of his life, the criterion by which he judged and evaluated his life. Dying was gain because he would be with Christ. It was that simple. "Your attitude should be the same as that of Christ Jesus" (2:5). What was that attitude? Jesus emptied Himself, left heaven's glory and entered into human experience, dwelt among us as a human being, and was perfectly obedient to God unto death.

"But whatever was to my profit I now consider loss for the sake of Christ. What is more, I consider everything a loss compared to the surpassing greatness of knowing Christ Jesus my Lord, for whose sake I have lost all things. I consider them rubbish, that I may gain Christ" (3:7–8). By comparison, everything else in life is insignificant. *Knowing Christ is better to me than position, stature, money, family, health. . . .* Fill in the blanks with whatever is producing stress for you. "I want to know Christ and the power of his resurrection and the fellowship of sharing in his sufferings, becoming like him in his death" (3:10).

The apostle had learned the lesson of the Sermon on the Mount: Don't be anxious about anything, but seek first God's Kingdom and righteousness, and everything else will be added to you.

One way to a stress-free life is having the right priorities. Put God first, and everything else falls into place. If He is not first, perhaps that's the cause of the stress! If He is first, you are able to enjoy the blessings of God without worshiping them, without seeing them as the source of your joy. You will be able to survive deprivation without railing against God and being cynical about life. This was the source of Paul's contentment. He had settled the matter of life's priorities, and he could cope with everything else on that basis.

Another coping mechanism Paul used is found in 1 Thessalonians 5:16–18. "Be joyful always; pray continually; give thanks in all circumstances, for this is God's will for you in Christ Jesus." It doesn't say, "For everything give thanks." Some things in life are horrible and God would be mocked if you thanked Him for them. The key word is *in.* You can face no circumstances, no matter how great or how bad, that make it impossible for you to give thanks to God for who He is. In fact, learning to thank God and praise Him for who He is in the midst of a mess is called "a sacrifice of praise." It is sacrificing your feelings and looking to God in the midst of tears and fears.

Summary

Paul's key to stress management is simply believing that God is who He is and will do what He says He will do. He doesn't leave us at the edge of the valleys of our lives and say, "See you later on the mountaintop." Paul had learned that key, lived it through all kinds of deprivation and glory, and was willing to accept whatever the hand of God had for him. "I can do all things through Christ, who strengthens me."

Understand this: Christ is in us through the power of His Holy Spirit. As a result, we can do anything God asks of us, painful or pleasurable. Learning how to cope with life through contentment and confidence, we will be able to manage the stresses of life that could affect our spiritual fitness.

Warm-Up Exercises

1. What causes the strongest stress reaction in you?

2. What would it take for you to be content in all circumstances?

3. How do you react to adversity? To success?

4. Can you apply Paul's coping mechanisms to your life?

Stretching

Memorize 1 Thessalonians 5:16–18 and try to do it daily: "Be joyful always; pray continually; give thanks in all circumstances, for this is God's will for you in Christ Jesus."

10

Body Building

Physical fitness is big business. All over the country, people seek personal trainers to work with them to develop certain muscles for maximum strength and visual effect. Thousands of gymnasiums have opened with equipment designed to pull and stretch and tone the muscles. Those who participate in these approaches realize they need help with the physical disciplines of their lives, necessary for the continued strength and suppleness of their bodies. They don't want to lose what they have, and they want to continue to improve, if at all possible.

But what about our spiritual lives? We can become out of shape spiritually much more quickly than we can physically! The Lord has provided a means for our spiritual bodies to be built up in needy areas. Of course, often we don't know which areas need the most improvement, as they are not as visible as our physical imperfections. That's why God has placed us in the Church, where others share a responsibility for our spiritual lives, and we share responsibility for theirs.

You know, the test of your life in the Spirit is not found in the number of spiritual, mystical experiences you might have. The validity of your spiritual life is found in the quality of your ordinary human relationships. The Spirit must make a difference *there,* or your walk in the Spirit is not real.

The apostle Paul makes a point of this in the book of Galatians:

> Since we live by the Spirit, let us keep in step with the Spirit. Let us not become conceited, provoking and envying each other.
>
> Brothers, if someone is caught in a sin, you who are spiritual should restore him gently. But watch yourself, or you also may be tempted. Carry each other's burdens, and in this way you will fulfill the law of Christ. If anyone thinks he is something when he is nothing, he deceives himself. Each one should test his own actions. Then he can take pride in himself, without comparing himself to somebody else, for each one should carry his own load.
>
> Galatians 5:25–6:5

This passage comes right after the familiar passage about the fruit of the Spirit. The connecting verse says, "Those who belong to Christ Jesus have crucified the sinful nature with its passions and desires" (verse 5:24). The fruit of the Spirit can't grow in a garden overgrown with the weeds of sin! How are the weeds pulled out? In Spirit-filled relationships.

The Lord Jesus has linked together our vertical relationship with God and our horizontal relationship with others. "Love God; love your neighbor as yourself," Jesus said. I don't know about your experience, but I've always found it much easier to love God than to love people. People have all sorts of things in them that make them difficult to love. But we have no choice; if we really want to love God, we must love others. And, Paul says, there are some clear ways to go about doing it.

Dependence on God

"Let us not become conceited, provoking and envying each other." What is conceit? It is an improper love of self, mixed with a bit of pride. It leads to provocation and envy, to trying constantly to prove ourselves better than the next person. Actually, conceit is probably based on a bit of insecurity, a feeling that we aren't all that certain we are that great, so we have to keep telling others and ourselves how wonderful we are. Some people have such low self-esteem that they are incapable of reaching out to others; they are consumed with their own problems. They haven't really heard in their hearts that God has redeemed them, that He has a plan for their lives, and that their lives can have dignity and significance—which is found only in Jesus. All of the stuff they can drum up about themselves and find within themselves won't make any difference.

In Romans 12, Paul says, "Do not think of yourself more highly than you ought, but rather think of yourself with sober judgment, in accordance with the measure of faith God has given you" (verse 3b). This doesn't mean that it glorifies the Lord to put ourselves down all the time. Self-degradation is a kind of perverse pride. It calls attention to oneself in a negative rather than a positive fashion. *Sober judgment* means "be realistic." If we are realistic, we are not conceited. If we are not conceited, we will not provoke one another or envy one another. You see, how we relate to others depends on how we see ourselves. Our behavior with another depends on the degree of security we have in the relationship; do we feel equal, superior, or inferior?

If you feel superior to someone, you may provoke her or challenge him in many ways. It's human nature to want to demonstrate superiority if we feel it. Think of the playground bullies you encountered as you grew up, and you'll get the sense of provocation that Paul is using here.

All of us can do at least one thing better than somebody else. You may be a better cook or a better typist or a better musician. But if our strengths are not used properly, not used in the power of the Spirit, for the benefit of others, we are allowing the gifts God gave us to lead us into sin.

At times everyone feels inferior. While there is always something we can do better, there is also something we can't do as well as someone else. This leads to envy. Think of a person just starting out at a gym—looking around at all of the muscular, trim bodies. It would be very hard to keep going at first! It requires a dose of "sober judgment" to see that nobody, except Jesus, has ever had it all together.

There's an interesting little statement that one could easily miss in the book of Deuteronomy. The Lord is speaking about driving the enemies of Israel from the Promised Land. He says, "I'm not going to let you drive out all of the enemies, because if you did, you would forget your dependence on Me." I believe that is true in our lives, as the Lord God seeks to stake His claim on us. The Lord wants us to be able to acknowledge our dependence on Him. Talk about "personal training"! This is personal training in righteousness! That's why we will never have it "all together" until we see Jesus face to face.

Gentle Restoration

Recognizing that we don't have it all together makes the next step possible. "If someone is caught in a sin, you who are spiritual should restore him gently." This tells what's to be done, who is to do it, and how it is to be done. It refers only to relationships within the Body of Christ; relationships with unbelievers are not included here. It is a matter of restoring a relationship within the Body that is damaged by sin. There are kinks to be worked out, injuries to be healed. This is a sensitive matter, especially in these days when some famous Christians have had lapses in the integrity of their walk with the Lord.

Any Christian can tell you from experience that there is a constant internal struggle to continue to be as God wants us to be. This is true for all of us for all of our lives. Walking in the Spirit is a day-by-day, minute-by-minute counting of ourselves as crucified with Christ. It's the spiritual counterpart to progressive resistance.

It is possible for Christians, when their guard is down, to lapse into serious sin that becomes scandalous and harmful to the Body of Christ. But it is also possible for the Body to respond in a way that is even more injurious to the cross of Christ. It is possible for the Body to respond in anger and judgment and horror. Individuals will even attack one another publicly, which becomes an occasion for those who oppose Christianity to say, "See, they're all a bunch of hypocrites, anyway." In that way the name and cause of Christ is damaged, in some cases irreparably.

What should be our reaction to brothers or sisters who fall? Paul says we are to restore them, gently. A Christian who has fallen into sin is already experiencing the condemnation of Satan, who will constantly seek to make that person feel as if he or she is beyond hope for doing such a terrible act that will never be forgiven. The person is sure he or she has destroyed his or her reputation and witness, if not career and life. Satan condemns. The Holy Spirit convicts. There is a difference. The conviction of the Holy Spirit is intended to lead us to repentance so that we might be restored to fellowship with Christ and with one another. Restored gently!

Restoration is the object. Who is to do it? "You who are spiritual," Paul says. Who does that mean? Somebody who is really moving in the Spirit. The tendency of our humanity is to be either too severe or not severe enough, to enlarge the offense or to minimize it. God never does that. He says we have to face our sin—see it as it is. It must be someone who is walking in the Spirit and can minister a tender love to a brother or sister who has strayed. One of the fruits of the Spirit is gentleness; here is where it comes to harvest.

"But watch yourself, or you also may be tempted," Paul says. Tempted? How? Well, tempted to handle the situation in the flesh. To deal with the sin of another from feelings of self-righteousness or righteous indignation. We are never to come crashing down on someone. We are to restore people gently and compassionately, recognizing that there but for the grace of God go you and I!

Burden Bearing

You know, sometimes when Christians have fallen, the last place they want to be is back in the church. They are ashamed and don't want to face those who know about their problems. It is our duty as Christians seeking to be fit for God's presence to make sure that we "carry each other's burdens, and in this way . . . fulfill the law of Christ." If we are willing to do that, to stand with persons as they are restored to fellowship, their burdens are lighter and their lives in the Church will have a whole new meaning. Talk about body-building exercises! The weight of carrying another's burdens will develop spiritual muscles we didn't even know we had.

It seems in a way to be a contradiction to the statement a few lines further down where Paul says, "Each one should carry his own load." But upon close examination, there is no contradiction, as two different words are used. The word for *burden* speaks of a heavy load; we are to help others with the heavy loads of life. That would be the kind of baggage you might find on a pack mule—too heavy for humans to bear.

The word for *load* translates to something like *backpack*. A backpack is something you fill and carry if you're going hiking or camping. Understand, I am not a great outdoorsman (about as primitive as I want to get is a nice room at the Marriott!), but I've known those who do these things. The point is, there are loads that we can carry with us. They are part of life, and we are expected to carry those alone. There are also loads with which we need help. We are to allow others to help us with these heavy burdens, and we are to help bear another's burdens. In this way we will fulfill the law of Christ. What is the law of Christ? To love God, and to love our neighbors as ourselves.

I want to take the next part of Paul's Galatians passage all in a piece, because it has to do with our attitudes as we bear one another's burdens, as we restore one another. Paul says, "If anyone thinks he is something when he is nothing, he deceives himself." In other words, "If you do perform a ministry, don't get a big head about it." This also applies to being helped. Don't say to yourself," I can handle it. I don't need help."

Paul continues, "Each one should test his own actions."

Attitude check: Why are you ministering? For the person, or for the person's gratitude toward you, and the possible credit it will bring you within the Body? Conversely, why are you refusing to be helped? Out of pride or shame or fear? Can't it all be done so that God can receive the glory? Paul hopes that to be the case and sums it up: "Then he can take pride in himself, without comparing himself to somebody else, for each one should carry his own load." Take a look at what God has been able to accomplish through you. If you feel you can boast, boast in what God has done.

God doesn't like our boasting, our pride. Jeremiah makes it very clear: "This is what the Lord says: 'Let not the wise man boast of his wisdom or the strong man boast of his strength or the rich man boast of his riches, but let him who boasts boast about this: that he understands and knows me, that I am the Lord, who exercises kindness, justice and righteousness on earth, for in these I delight,' declares the Lord" (Jeremiah 9:23–24).

Summary

How do we build up our spiritual bodies to be fit for God's presence? By walking in the Spirit in human relationships without conceit, provocation, or envy. By seeking to restore others to Christ and to relationships within the body in gentleness, taking care that we are not led into sin in the process. By knowing ourselves well and by bearing others' burdens. And by doing these body-building exercises tirelessly. Paul exhorts, "Let us not become weary in doing good, for at the proper time we will reap a harvest if we do not give up. Therefore, as we have opportunity, let us do good to all people, especially to those who belong to the family of believers" (Galatians 6:9–10). By building up the Body of Christ, we build up our own spiritual bodies, making them increasingly fit for God's presence.

Warm-Up Exercises

1. How do you feel the relationships in your life reflect the work of the Holy Spirit in you?

2. Do you tend to build yourself up or tear yourself down?

3. Do you know someone who might be restored to Christ and His Church? Is the Holy Spirit leading you to do it?

Stretching

Memorize Jeremiah 9:23–24. Make the exercising of kindness, justice, and righteousness a part of your daily program toward spiritual fitness: "This is what the Lord says: 'Let not the wise man boast of his wisdom or the strong man boast of his strength or the rich man boast of his riches, but let him who boasts boast about this: that he understands and knows me, that I am the Lord, who exercises kindness, justice and righteousness on earth, for in these I delight,' declares the Lord."

11

Ready, Willing, and Able

Throughout the preceding chapters, we have been seeking to understand the means to spiritual fitness. I want to end this book with an explanation of the desired end, the reason our spiritual fitness is so essential—why it is important to start it, build on it, and maintain it.

What are we talking about when we refer to being fit for God's presence? Making ourselves fit for God's presence means that we are actively seeking to be ready, willing, and able to enter into a precious relationship with God.

Metaphors of Relationship

Scripture uses many metaphors to draw pictures of this relationship, just as I've used fitness metaphors. A careful study of these biblical metaphors reveals many important truths about the Lord and about our relationship with Him.

For example, Psalm 23 says that God is our Shepherd, and we are His sheep. A shepherd is one who cares for a flock. A shepherd leads his flock, and the Lord leads us. The psalmist says that the Lord "leads me in paths of righteousness for his name's sake" (verse 3, RSV). This means that He has a stake in where we go, how we live our lives. That's part of the nature of our relationship to Him. Verse 2 says He "leads me beside quiet waters"— quiet waters, so we can drink and be refreshed. Sheep can't drink from a rushing river.

Shepherds also protect their flocks. "Though I walk through the valley of the shadow of death . . . you are with me" (verse 4). We are to understand that we get through hard times because He is with us.

There is something to be learned from that metaphor from the other side of it, too: We are sheep. Sheep are not particularly intelligent animals. They are stubborn and need a lot of guidance. They wander off and are not even aware that they are lost. The prophet Isaiah says, "We all, like sheep, have gone astray" (53:6a).

Another image used to describe the relationship between God and His people is: The Lord is our Father; we are His children. This metaphor is used all the way through the Bible. In Deuteronomy 8 God says He will discipline us as a father disciplines his child. In Proverbs 3 we are told not to be discouraged when we are chastised, for God chastens all He receives as His children. Hebrews 12 says that just as we have had earthly parents discipline us to guide us in the right way, so the Lord disciplines us for our good, that we might share in His holiness. Scripture also refers to God as a Father who doesn't forget us, who cares for us.

What do we see in ourselves as God's children? We see that we are loved, desired, welcomed to the family. We are born into the family of God and we grow through various stages of development. God rejoices in our triumphs and agonizes with us in our pain. He provides for our daily needs and plans for our futures, and most of all, He has made the sacrifice necessary for our eternal life.

Another metaphor is in Jeremiah 18, where the Lord is the Potter, and we are the clay. From this metaphor, found in both the Old and New Testaments, we could draw the wrong conclusion, as clay is relatively inert in the hands of a potter. But you and I are able to resist or yield to the shaping God seeks to do in our lives. If we yield, we will find that our lives, however broken and fragmented,

are able to be remade into vessels of beauty and usefulness.

As clay, we need to remember that part of the process of
becoming a useful vessel is "being thrown"—clay is
thrown with great force again and again to get the air
bubbles and imperfections out. This is not a pleasant
process, but the potter is in complete control; he knows
the results he desires and the usefulness that will be
produced.

Remember the metaphor in John's Gospel used in that
little song "He Is the Vine, We Are the Branches"? From
that metaphor we learn that if we are cut off from God, we
cannot live and bear fruit.

There is one metaphor that I want to examine closely as
I draw this book to a close. It speaks of the relationship
between God and His people as no other. It opens for us
the very heart of God, that we might see what is in the
depths of His being when He thinks of us. It also speaks
of the reason we would want to be fit for His presence—
because we will be presented to Him as His Bride.

Your Maker Is Your Husband

Scripture says that God wants to relate to us as a
husband does to his wife. The Lord God and His people
have a marriage relationship. In Isaiah 54:5 we read: "For
your Maker is your husband—the Lord Almighty is his
name—the Holy One of Israel is your Redeemer; he is
called the God of all the earth."

If we thought of Him as Maker alone, we might see in
Him great and infinite creative power. But when we
understand that this infinite, creative God wishes to relate
Himself to us as intimately as a husband to a wife, we can
understand more of His heart and the nature of His
commitment to us.

Marriage is a two-way commitment—each making a
commitment to the other. I'd like to have us let the reality

of this relationship sink into our hearts and lives, for we deal with a God who loves us, and because He loves us He has exposed Himself to the possibility of pain.

How can we hurt God? By rejecting Him, rebuffing Him, refusing His love. I'm not even sure that words are capable of explaining this.

Why do you think God loves us? Why is it that He has chosen to bind Himself forever to the likes of you and me? I think it can be explained only in terms of the nature of God, because God is Love. There is something about love that desires to give: "For God so loved the world that he gave his one and only Son" (John 3:16a). Perhaps the nature of God, being Love, required an object for His love. It is certain that He doesn't need us; we will find no lack in Him. This is not so with human marriage. Our mates are often those who possess qualities we do not have. God is complete and infinite, yet He called forth a creation upon whom He could lavish His love.

Courtship

Like any marriage, the one between God and His people is preceded by a period of courtship. All the way through the Bible we find a God who seeks us out, a God who endeavors to draw us unto Himself with the call of love, so that we respond not because of fear of His power and might, but because His words of love are drawing us closer to Him.

Scripture is a love letter. It tells of a God who loves us and calls us to Himself. Again and again, we find reference to this courtship in which God seeks to win us, such as this passage from Hosea: "Therefore I am now going to allure her; I will lead her into the desert and speak tenderly to her" (2:14). Why? He tells us in verse 16: " 'In that day,' declares the Lord, 'you will call me "my husband"; you will no longer call me "my master." ' " God wants to love us, not rule us.

Cinderella Story

One of the most powerful passages in all of Scripture using this metaphor is in Ezekiel. Here, Israel, before she was even a tribe or a nation, is referred to as the object of God's love.

> "This is what the Sovereign Lord says to Jerusalem: Your ancestry and birth were in the land of the Canaanites; your father was an Amorite and your mother a Hittite. [God was pointing out the poverty of the origins of His chosen people.] On the day you were born your cord was not cut, nor were you washed with water to make you clean, nor were you rubbed with salt or wrapped in cloth. No one looked on you with pity or had compassion enough to do any of these things for you. Rather, you were thrown out into the open field, for on the day you were born you were despised. [Here God is speaking of their ejection from Egypt.]
> "Then I passed by and saw you kicking about in your blood, and as you lay there in your blood I said to you, 'Live!' I made you grow like a plant of the field. You grew up and developed and became the most beautiful of jewels. Your breasts were formed and your hair grew, you who were naked and bare.
> "Later I passed by, and when I looked at you and saw that you were old enough for love, I spread the corner of my garment over you and covered your nakedness. I gave you my solemn oath and entered into a covenant with you, declares the Sovereign Lord, and you became mine."
>
> Ezekiel 16:3–8

This is the "Cinderella" story of the Bible—God taking one who was rejected, and nurturing, cleansing, purifying, and clothing her. Covering with a garment was a sign of protection. A woman without a husband needed a male relative to protect her. In the story of Ruth you see the example of Boaz covering her with his garment, signifying that he would be responsible for her. But not only did God pledge His protection to His people; He gave His solemn oath of betrothal. He entered into a covenant like marriage with His people.

> "I bathed you with water and washed the blood from you and put ointments on you. I clothed you with an embroi-dered dress and put leather sandals on you. I dressed you in fine linen and covered you with costly garments. I adorned you with jewelry: I put bracelets on your arms and a necklace around your neck, and I put a ring on your nose, earrings on your ears and a beautiful crown on your head. So you were adorned with gold and silver; your clothes were of fine linen and costly fabric and embroidered cloth. Your food was fine flour, honey and olive oil. You became very beautiful and rose to be a queen. And your fame spread among the nations on account of your beauty, because the splendor I had given you made your beauty perfect, declares the Sovereign Lord."   verses 9–14

God washed His people—as Jesus did the Church, cleansing it by water and the Word. He raised them to the level of royalty; we are a chosen race, a royal priesthood. He clothed them in glory, in fine garments, that they might be beautiful. Jesus clothed us with splendor and might that we might be a chaste bride before Him forever.

Think of this in terms of your own relationship with the Lord. Have you ever thought of Jesus as Lover of your soul? As the Pursuer, the One seeking you so that you might be His, not as a slave, but as His beloved bride?

Eternal Marriage

The relationship God offers us is permanent. It's in-tended to be forever. It's a relationship that does not change as the years go by. In Hosea we read God's pledge: "I will betroth you to me forever; I will betroth you in righteous-ness and justice, in love and compassion. I will betroth you in faithfulness, and you will acknowledge the Lord" (2:19–

20). A forever relationship of love is something we can hardly imagine. God will never waver in His commitment to us. It is not conditional on our response to Him.

Yet the love of God is often an unrequited love. As a matter of fact, the book of Hosea is a story of a prophet living out his teaching. He was married to Gomer, a prostitute. He knew her background, yet he married her and clothed her beautifully. She turned from him and lavished her affections on others who came along. Then she left him, sought others, and was rejected by one after another. And all through this, Hosea was paying for her needs, her food and clothing.

The word of the Lord came to Hosea, when his wife was reduced to slavery and about to be auctioned off. "Hosea, I want you to go down to the slave market and buy your own wife back to you. Forgive her and restore her to a place of honor beside you."

Hosea did just that. In this we see the need for God sending His Son as a ransom for us. You see, we were already His, but we had wandered away and rejected Him. He had to ransom us back.

We can see the heart of God anguishing over our faithlessness in Hosea 11. Put your own name in the place of Ephraim and Israel. "How can I give you up, Ephraim? How can I hand you over, Israel? . . . My heart is changed within me; all my compassion is aroused. I will not carry out my fierce anger, nor devastate Ephraim again. For I am God, and not man—the Holy One among you. I will not come in wrath" (verses 8–9).

This is the love that sent Jesus to the cross to buy us back to Himself. The story of your relationship and mine to the Lord is as a faithless wife, at best. When we allow ourselves to come back into His arms, to take our place beside Him, we will know something of the grace, kindness, love, and mercy of our Lord God!

One of the euphemisms for having a relationship with the Lord is "knowing the Lord." I often hear people ask,

"How long have you known the Lord?" This is not the kind of "knowing" that we might use with one another, as in, "I've known Susan since she was six years old." The term *know*, as referring to the Lord's knowledge of us and us of Him, is as in Genesis: Adam "knew" his wife and she conceived a son. It is the most intimate, personal relationship possible. It is meant to be completely open, completely honest, nothing held back and nothing hidden. God chooses to reveal Himself to us in that fashion and desires our open response to Him in that same way.

I want to make one final point. This relationship is not one of force. It is not rape. It is a love relationship, not one of abuse. God stands at the door and waits for our invitation to love. He woos and courts us, washes and cleanses us, makes us ready and fit for His loving presence. He then waits for us to say, "Come." He never violates that freedom. He cannot make us love Him. He waits for us to respond.

Summary

Do you know the Lord in that sense? Have you opened your heart to respond to His love? Are you a wife fit for His arms? Whether you are a man or a woman, the analogy is the same. Are you a bride washed in the blood of Christ, clothed in His power and glory, fit for His presence?

Warm-Up Exercises

1. Think about your own relationship with God. Create a metaphor that describes it.

2. Have you caused God pain through rejection or faithlessness? Seek reconciliation!

3. What has the Lord done in your life to draw you closer to Him?

Stretching

Memorize Hosea 2:19–20 and know it is a promise God intends to keep: "I will betroth you to me forever; I will betroth you in righteousness and justice, in love and compassion. I will betroth you in faithfulness, and you will acknowledge the Lord."